C0-AZJ-420

TAX-DEFERRED INVESTING

Using Pre-Tax Dollars for After-Tax Profit

MICHAEL C. THOMSETT

John Wiley & Sons, Inc.

New York • Chichester • Brisbane • Toronto • Singapore

In recognition of the importance of preserving what has been written, it is a policy of John Wiley & Sons, Inc. to have books of enduring value published in the United States printed on acid-free paper, and we exert our best efforts to that end.

Copyright © 1991 by John Wiley & Sons, Inc.

All rights reserved. Published simultaneously in Canada.

Reproduction or translation of any part of this work beyond that permitted by Section 107 or 108 of the 1976 United States Copyright Act without the permission of the copyright owner is unlawful. Requests for permission or further information should be addressed to the Permissions Department, John Wiley & Sons, Inc.

This publication is designed to provide accurate and authoritative information in regard to the subject matter covered. It is sold with the understanding that the publisher is not engaged in rendering legal, accounting, or other professional services. If legal advice or other expert assistance is required, the services of a competent professional person should be sought.

From a Declaration of Principles jointly adopted by a Committee of the American Bar Association and a Committee of Publishers.

Library of Congress Cataloging-in-Publication Data

Thomsett, Michael C.
    Tax-deferred investing : using pre-tax dollars for after-tax
profit / by Michael C. Thomsett.
        p.   cm.
    Includes index.
    ISBN 0-471-53230-4 (cloth)
    1. Tax shelters—United States.   2. Investments—Taxation—
United States.   I. Title.
HJ4653.T38T48 1991
343.7305'23—dc20   91-6408
[347.303523]   CIP

Printed in the United States of America.

91 92 10 9 8 7 6 5 4 3 2 1

CONTENTS

SECTION V: Tax Rules for Investors

SECTION VI: Launching Your New Strategy

INTRODUCTION

Pay Now or Pay Later

Would you rather your earnings were taxable or tax-deferred? Although the answer might seem obvious, the question is more complex than it first seems.

Tax deferral is nothing more than a delay of liability. Rather than paying tax on investment profits from one year to the next, you put off your payment date until a bond matures or until you retire and begin withdrawing money from an individual retirement account.

Deferral is attractive for a number of reasons. First, if you are using tax-deferral techniques to save for retirement, chances are you will be in a lower tax bracket when you begin withdrawing your funds. By timing withdrawals, you will also be able to control both your income level and your tax liability from one year to the next.

Second, if your tax-deferred earnings are compounding each year (see Chapter 1), the overall effect is to increase the return on your money. You will probably be required to leave the principal and each year's earnings on deposit, since most forms of tax-deferred investing require that the amount invested not be removed. So compounding is a built-in advantage in a number of tax-deferred investments.

Third, tax deferral is ideally suited to long-term goals. These may include paying for a child's college education, saving for retirement, or buying real estate in the distant future. Since you can choose from a variety of investments, you can control the timing of the deferral period.

Certain investments are sheltered from year-to-year taxes for a num-

1

ber of reasons. Individual retirement accounts and other qualified plans contain deferral provisions as a matter of law to encourage people to plan ahead and save. In savings bonds, deferral helps offset a relatively low rate of return. And some investments, such as real estate, achieve deferral by growth in market value over time. In each case, you control your own tax liability by deciding when to sell and when to report the tax.

Many forms of tax-deferred investing offer exceptional advantages. Buying your own home is a good example. The home's market value may grow by $100,000 over the next 10 to 20 years. This increased home equity is not taxed, however, until you sell the home. Even then, you can defer the profit indefinitely by buying another home of equal or greater value within two years.

Savings bonds offer a different advantage. Interest is paid at a compounded rate, and the entire profit is deferred until you cash in the bonds. Most other bonds do not pay compound interest, and payments are taxed each year. Savings bonds also come with a guaranteed minimum rate of return, and their safety is guaranteed by the full faith and credit of the U.S. government. For these reasons they are among the safest of all investments.

These examples show that tax advantages are still in abundant supply. Tax regulations have been massively changed to eliminate abusive tax shelters; however, economically sound, substantial investments can still be found.

Tax deferral, however, should be only one of the points to consider when comparing one investment with another. In some instances, a taxable investment may be more advantageous to you than one that is tax-deferred. Risks may vary, and your tax status could be the determining factor in selecting one investment over another. Thus your decision should not be based solely on the percentage rate offered; you should also consider your tax bracket, your willingness to assume risk, and your long-term purpose in wanting to invest money. Too many people fail to think these things through and therefore make their choice prematurely.

All of the information in this book is based on the premise that every investor is different. In explaining the various methods of tax deferral, it continually emphasizes that you first need to define investment priorities for yourself and your family. A number of illustrations and examples are included, and important words and phrases are defined in the glossary at the end of the book, as well as in the text as they appear.

This book also presents a number of checklists to help you establish priorities, identify the advantages of each form of tax deferral, and make a selection best suited to your own circumstances. This makes it easy for you to quickly find that part of the book most relevant to the decisions you are facing today and to quickly identify the most important questions, key points, or features of any one tax-deferred investment.

The purpose of this book is to describe the workings of tax deferral. However, to repeat, deferral is only one strategy among many. You will succeed in reaching your goals by selecting appropriate strategies and investment products, and to do this you must know what you want to achieve and where to find the most suitable answers. There are no "sure things," no easy ways to get rich in the market, no risk-free investments. With definition, review, and sound management, you will achieve your goals. Tax deferral may play a critical role in your success.

SECTION ONE

Strategy and Action

CHAPTER 1

The New Tax Realities

Tax increases have never been popular ideas. Elected representatives do not want to be perceived as favoring higher taxes because they fear the voters will take revenge in the next election. Thus, politicians prefer ideas like "revenue enhancement" over the dreaded new or higher tax.

In the mid-1980s, this dilemma gave rise to the idea of tax simplification. The *Tax Reform Act of 1986* eliminated multiple tax brackets, replacing them with only three. But the act was far from simple. Anyone who has prepared a tax return since 1986 knows that taxes now are more complicated than ever. And Congress isn't through yet. Change has become the norm in taxation. The 1990s started out as a decade preoccupied with federal budget deficits and yet more tax reform on the horizon.

The Effects of Tax Reform

The new restrictions have changed the way we all invest. Before the recent tax reforms, investors looked for tax advantages. Now, you need to be aware of tax consequences arising from the timing and selection of investments. Although the brackets have been simplified, virtually every other aspect of taxation has been complicated, and many advantages you had in the past have been eliminated by tax reform.

Everyone needs to pay careful attention to tax reform. For example, the massive 1986 act was never called a tax increase; indeed, the maximum tax bracket was reduced. However, with the elimination of many deductions previously allowed and with restrictions on many previous tax advantages, the result of tax reform, for many, is a higher annual tax bill. The 1986 act had deep and widespread ramifications for all investors. The major changes that affect you as an investor are as follows:

1. *Elimination of favorable capital gains rates.* A *capital gain* is a profit on the sale of a capital asset, which includes stocks and bonds, mutual fund shares, and real estate. Not included are forms of income from investments, such as interest, dividends, or rent. The distinction is between profit (capital gain) and income earned and paid each year.

   Under the tax rules prior to the 1986 act, only 40 percent of a long-term capital gain was taxed; the rest was completely free from taxation. To receive this favorable treatment, it was only necessary to hold on to investments long enough to make them qualify as long-term.

   Understandably, with this benefit it was a great advantage to avoid turning over investments too quickly. A discount of 60 percent on investment taxable income could not be ignored but that meant holding on longer. The 1986 law eliminated the favorable treatment, so that all capital gains—both short-term and long-term—became fully taxed.

   Nevertheless, the distinction between long-term and short-term has been left intact in the tax regulations. In the future, the rules may be modified again. The favorable treatment of long-term gains may be reinstated, or at least taxed at a modified, reduced rate.

2. *Limitation of passive losses.* A *passive investment* is one in which you do not participate materially. For example, if you invest money in a program managed by someone else, that is a passive activity. The public limited partnerships so popular in the 1970s and early 1980s were passive investments and became extremely popular as *tax shelters,* or ways to avoid taxation. To eliminate the abusive sheltering of income, Congress enacted rules limiting passive losses.

   Under current tax rules, passive losses can be used only to offset gains from passive activities in the same year. They cannot be claimed against other investment income (interest and dividends) or against salaries or self-employment income. This change did away with the problem of investors claiming large passive losses and eliminating taxes even when their other income was quite high. It used to be possible to claim such large passive losses that investments were made purely for their tax advantages, not for their underlying economic value. These *abusive tax shelters* were an advantage to people in the higher tax brackets, for whom a little year-end planning could mean elimination of all or most of the annual tax.

3. *Limit on deduction of interest.* In the past, investors were willing to leverage their capital to increase the amount of money placed in investments. Part of the reasoning was that interest would be deductible on the tax return. However, the 1986 rules included a phasing out of the personal interest deduction; now, interest other than on your home mortgage cannot be claimed as an itemized deduction.

You may still deduct home mortgage interest, but there is a limit. The amount borrowed cannot be greater than either the fair market value or the basis in the property. The *basis* is the cost plus extras paid in. Interest on mortgage debt above these levels is not deductible. With exchanges of property, many individuals have deferred gains and have a very low basis in their residences. This means that for many the maximum deduction of mortgage interest is severely limited.

4. *Changes in IRA deductibility.* Before the 1986 act, anyone with earned income (from salaries or self-employment, for example) was allowed to contribute as much as $2,000 per year in an *individual retirement account (IRA)* (see Chapter 6 for more detailed information on IRAs). The IRA came with two very attractive features. First, the amount placed in the IRA was deducted from gross income; thus, up to $2,000 per year was tax deferred. Second, all earnings in the IRA account were deferred until funds were withdrawn. Investing in an IRA was a wise move. For example, if the effective tax rate was 40 percent of taxable income, a $2,000 investment in an IRA produced an immediate tax reduction of $800—even before those funds began earning interest or dividends.

Under current rules, you may still put up to $2,000 per year in an IRA, and the deferral of tax on earnings still applies. However, the amount contributed to the account each year is not necessarily deducted from gross income. If you participate in an employer-maintained retirement account during the year, you may or may not be allowed to deduct your IRA contribution, depending on your income level.

For single people who do participate in another retirement plan, the IRA contribution is fully deductible on income up to $25,000; the benefit is reduced when income ranges up to $35,000, and it's eliminated altogether above that level. For married couples, full deduction is allowed on incomes up to $40,000, partial deduction is allowed for incomes up to $50,000, and the deduction is eliminated for incomes above that level.

Anyone who does not participate in another plan is allowed to deduct the full IRA contribution from gross income, up to the maximum: $2,000 or income for the year, whichever is less.

Although the tax-deferred earnings in the IRA continue to offer a significant benefit, the popularity of IRA investing has diminished in recent years. Without the immediate tax incentive, many people are not interested in long-term deferral by itself. Deferral may present enough of an advantage for many investors. However, there is one major disadvantage to the deductible IRA: money must be left in the account for many years; withdrawing it early means an immediate tax and a 10 percent penalty as well.

Other Important Changes

Elimination of tax shelters, preferential treatment of capital gains, and IRA benefits were only one side of the Tax Reform Act of 1986. Several other changes restricted the deductions you are allowed to claim on your individual tax return—meaning that, for many, the lower brackets translate to a higher tax.

Itemized deductions for medical and miscellaneous expenses were reduced by a percentage of gross income. So the higher your annual income, the more medical or miscellaneous expense you need to claim a deduction.

Income averaging was repealed in the 1986 act. Before that, if you had widely fluctuating incomes from one year to the next, you were given a tax break in unusually high income years: you could pay tax at the average rate applicable over a five-year period. That provision is no longer available.

Rules for the *alternative minimum tax* (*AMT*) were changed as well. The AMT is an additional tax applied to people with higher incomes and *preference items*, certain tax-exempt forms of income or special deductions. These items include accelerated depreciation on investment property, excess fair market value of stock options, tax-exempt interest on some municipal bonds, charitable contributions of property that has appreciated in value since its acquisition, and several specialized deductions. In calculating AMT, you must also add back the standard deduction to taxable income; if you do not, and if you itemize, many of those deductions are taken away. The AMT is computed in comparison with the usual tax, and the higher of the two must be paid. The purpose is to reduce the benefits of a large number of tax-sheltering strategies.

Some provisions of the 1986 law favored lower-income families while shifting the tax burden into higher-income levels. The alternative minimum tax was one provision that achieved this. At the same time, both standard deduction and personal exemption levels were increased, a change which benefits those who do not itemize or who have a larger-than-average number of dependants.

As complicated as taxes were before the new law, they are far more complicated today. The reduction in the number of tax brackets and the ceiling on the maximum tax rate will not make a significant difference in tax liability for most middle-income families. Before the 1986 law was passed, the maximum rate was 50 percent of taxable income. Since 1987, the highest marginal rate has been 33 percent. However, under the old system, there were many ways for higher-income people to shelter their income. With the elimination of tax shelters as an investing and tax strategy, an entire industry of abusive investments has been rendered obsolete. At the same time, many long-standing deductions (such as sales tax and nonmortgage interest) are no longer deductible. So lower tax rates are offset by fewer deductions, which means higher taxes for some and very small differences for others.

The ramifications of taxes and tax reform are far too complex for the scope of this book. This chapter has highlighted some of the important effects of recent changes on investors only to stress that taxation is a very important consideration in planning and selecting investments. It would be unrealistic to project future value in isolation; you need to consider the year-to-year tax consequences of your decision and to plan for the future with taxes in mind. And because tax reform is an ongoing activity in Congress, you also need to check with a professional who is familiar with tax rules for investors, keep up to date on new changes, and plan with those changes in mind.

Changing Your Approach

The tax question is often used by financial planners and salespeople. The argument is made in several ways. For example, you may be encouraged to borrow money secured by home equity to free up investment funds. The interest will be deductible; thus, going into debt is acceptable, so the argument goes. Or, you may be advised to put money into municipal bonds, which are exempt from taxation. That might be advisable, depending on your income and tax status, but it may be the wrong move if avoidance of taxes is not your primary concern. Avoiding taxes should never be the sole motive for making an investment decision. It is certainly important, and it must be taken into account when estimating the real rate of return. However, it is equally important to compare risks and to keep your personal goals in mind.

Many individual investors react to advice without asking the right questions and without first defining what they need and want. For example, your stockbroker calls and suggests buying shares in a "hot" company. Of course, the broker calls all of his or her clients with the same advice, so the idea is not tailored to your particular interests. Or, you respond to an advertisement for a mutual fund and buy shares, not because the fund's investment objectives match your goals, but because it sounds safe and secure and has yielded a high rate of return in the past.

A more logical approach is to begin with the premise that you have specific short-term and long-term goals. Given your financial status, you then need to determine the level of risk appropriate for yourself. There is an unavoidable relationship between risk and reward. The greater the potential income, the greater the risk.

Next, the attributes of each investment dictate whether or not it is appropriate for you. For example, suppose you accept risk in the form of illiquidity by selecting an investment that makes it difficult to get your money back within the next 10 years. If you think you might need that money in five years, then the investment is obviously inappropriate.

By defining risk levels in the context of your own goals, you have already narrowed down the selection process. Any investment that violates the standards you set for yourself can be quickly eliminated. This does away with the uncertainty and doubt that many investors face when having to decide from among a number of choices.

As a final step, the comparison between two or more choices should be made with taxes in mind. Taxes should not be the sole basis for the decision, only a gauge for ensuring that the investments are properly compared. For example, you might compare a taxable bond currently yielding 10 percent per year with a Series EE bond paying 7.5 percent. The taxable bond yields more; however, there is no compounding, and income will be taxed each year. It may also present you with higher risks than the EE bond. So the difference in yield cannot be limited to a comparison between 10 percent and 7.5 percent. The risks, compounding, and tax status of each investment may make them much closer in ultimate yield than they seem.

The selection process is summarized in four steps.

1. *Set investment goals.* Always begin the process of selecting investments by identifying your individual goals and setting the target

date, the time in the future when you will need to put your hands on your money.

2. *Compare risk levels.* Do not limit your evaluation to historical rates of return. First of all, the past is not always a reliable indicator of future performance; moreover, the differences in risk will be reflected in the yield.

You may chase higher-yielding investments if you can live with the risk of losing your money. However, you may also conclude that a lower yield is preferable when you simply cannot afford the exposure to loss.

3. *Examine attributes.* Use attributes of each investment to narrow the field of selection. For example, if you need a high degree of liquidity, you will be drawn toward investments in which you can get your money whenever you need it. Individual retirement accounts, limited partnerships, and long-term certificates of deposit are not appropriate if you will need the money back in the near future. Once you understand the attributes of an investment, your decision becomes much easier.

ACTION CHECKLIST

Protecting Your Tax Position

1. Keep track of new tax law changes.
2. Learn the passive loss rules.
3. Find out the status of profit and loss before investing money. Avoid accumulating any passive losses you cannot use.
4. Avoid all nondeductible interest expenses.
5. Invest through your IRA to defer gains on profits.
6. Determine your status for the alternative minimum tax.
7. Don't believe arguments aimed at making decisions just to avoid taxes.
8. Ask questions of advisers. Don't make any decisions until you get answers.
9. Base decisions on personal goals and risk tolerance, never on this year's tax benefits or consequences.
10. Plan ahead for the entire year. Be aware of your tax status at all times.

4. *Compare on an after-tax basis.* As the final step, make sure your evaluation of each investment is made with tax benefits or consequences in mind. A taxable 10 percent yield may be comparable to a tax-free or tax-deferred yield that is much lower—all depending on your current and future income. Your comparisons are valid only when you have adjusted yields with taxes in mind.

Chapter 2 includes a more detailed examination of the selection process.

How Deferral Benefits You

Once you have compared investments that are taxed this year with those that are deferred, you can estimate future growth potential. This is important for judging future value, and it is necessary for reaching your goals. For example, if you are saving for a child's college education in 15 or 20 years, you will need to understand the future value of the investment: not just by what it yields each year, but also with the tax consequences in mind.

Since deferral is nothing more than a delay in payment of taxes, the benefit may seem minimal. What is the difference between paying 33 percent today and paying 33 percent a few years later? Two points should be made concerning this question. First, many people save in tax-deferred accounts with retirement in mind. It can be safely assumed that your tax bracket will be lower after retirement; thus, the income you recieve once you have stopped working probably will be taxed at a lower rate. That is one important benefit to deferral. Second, when tax-deferred investments are allowed to grow at compounded rates, the overall result is greater profits, even after a future tax liability is paid. With *compound interest*, the earnings grow each year, because interest for each period is added to the basis. With *simple interest*, the same payment is made each period. Your money won't grow.

> *Example:* You want to place $1,000 in an account this year. You plan to retire in 25 years, when you will withdraw the funds. Assuming that the money will earn an annual rate of 9 percent every year, how will your money grow?

Figure 1-1 compares a taxable with a tax-deferred 9 percent growth rate. We assume that the interest earned will all be left on account to grow at a compound rate. The calculation reflects quarterly compounding of interest and is based on an assumed tax rate of 33 percent.

$1,000 investment, single deposit
9% interest compounded quarterly
33% tax rate

YEAR	TAXABLE	DEFERRED
5	$ 1,347	$ 1,561
10	1,814	2,435
15	2,443	3,800
20	3,291	5,930
25	4,432	9,254

FIGURE 1-1 Compound Interest, Single Deposit

What happens if, at the end of 25 years, you withdraw the entire fund worth $9,254? Since $1,000 was deposited at the beginning, the profit from this investment is $8,254. If that is taxed at 33 percent, the tax liability will be $2,724. The *after-tax profit* (the portion left after taxes are paid) is then computed as follows:

Total interest	$8,254
Less 33% tax	2,724
After-tax profit	$5,530

Compare this with the profit in the taxable account. The investment grew to $4,432 after taxes were paid each year. Subtracting the initial $1,000 deposit produces an income of $3,432, which can then be compared with the tax-deferred income:

After-tax profit:	
Tax-deferred	$5,530
Taxable	3,432
Difference	$2,098

This example shows how a comparison should be made between taxable and tax-deferred investments. The compound interest in the tax-deferred account translates to higher after-tax profits. To match these profits, the taxable account would have to earn a substantially higher rate of return, or yield (which would also mean higher risks). To estimate the required *pre-tax yield* of the taxable account, divide the tax-deferred yield by the percentage left after taxes. In this example, the tax-deferred yield is 9 percent, and the after-tax percentage is 67 percent (100 less 33).

$$\frac{9\%}{67\%} = 13.43\%$$

Thus to match a tax-deferred yield of 9 percent, you would need an investment paying pre-tax interest at 13.43 percent

Pre-tax yield	13.43%
Less 33% tax	4.44
After-tax yield	8.99%

This raises a critical question: How much more risk would you need to assume at 13.44 percent than you would at 9 percent? Because risk and reward are directly related, this issue cannot be ignored. Seeking a higher yield would change the entire character of your investment and would also change your risk profile.

Example: You could obtain a 9 percent return within your individual retirement account, where all earnings are tax-deferred. (The funds are placed in long-term certificates of deposit.) You would like to match this return outside the IRA. However, in comparing available investments, you discover that the only choices offering pre-tax yields above 13 percent are far too risky. Not only would your capital be exposed to possible loss; the rate itself is only historical and that is not guaranteed in the future.

The risk comparison is not limited to the initial rate of return; you also need to consider the long-term risk. The previous example was based on the deposit of a single sum at the beginning of a 25-year period. The comparison between tax-deferred and taxable is even more dramatic when a regular series of deposits are made. Another example shows how the tax-deferred benefits of compounding can make a large difference over time.

Example: You have decided to deposit $250 per quarter in a retirement account yielding 9 percent per year. You will accumulate your retirement funds over the next 25 years. Assuming a 9 percent return compounded quarterly and an annual tax rate of 33 percent, how would a taxable account compare with a tax-deferred account?

Figure 1-2 gives you the results of this comparison. The tax-deferred account will grow to a much higher level with a series of deposits. The after-tax profits are computed as follows. The total deposited over the 25 years is $25,000. Deduct this from the fund's value ($91,712) to arrive at the interest earned. The answer is $66,712, which can then be used to make an after-tax comparison:

Total interest	$66,712
Less 33% tax	22,015
After-tax profit	$44,697

The total of the taxable account, $57,201, is reduced by the same $25,000 in deposits, so total after-tax earnings from that account are $32,201. Compare this with the after-tax profits of the tax-deferred account:

After-tax profit:	
Tax-deferred	$44,697
Taxable	32,201
Difference	$12,201

In this example, the tax-deferred return is $12,201 greater than an equivalent taxable return at the same rate.

Again, you would need to earn a pre-tax rate of 13.44 percent each year to equal the tax-deferred yield. In a tax-deferred account (such as an IRA), it might be fairly easy to earn 9 percent over the long term. However, it will not always be possible to earn the higher rate each and every

$1,000 investment per year ($250 per quarter)
9% interest compounded quarterly
33% tax rate

YEAR	TAXABLE	DEFERRED
5	$ 5,781	$ 6,228
10	13,567	15,947
15	24,054	31,113
20	38,178	54,779
25	57,201	91,712

FIGURE 1-2 Compound Interest, Series of Deposits

A C T I O N   C H E C K L I S T

Long-Term Deferral Planning

1. Define your long-term goals.
2. Examine investments with your goals in mind.
3. Compare taxable and tax-deferred returns with similar risk levels to find the best deal.
4. Calculate returns on an after-tax basis. Then evaluate comparative risks.

---

year, for several reasons. First, the higher rate will probably involve placing the initial investment at risk; if the value declines, the investment will not keep pace with the lower, tax-deferred yield. Second, changing market conditions could make the higher rate unattainable. Third, the interest rate and capital risk will be constant.

Watching For the Pitfalls

Too much emphasis on taxes could distract you, not only from maintaining the appropriate risk profile, but also from reaching your long-term goals. One of the dangers in investing is becoming obsessed with today's profits and forgetting where you intend to end up.

The tax issue should be managed within the framework of your goal. If your entire portfolio is structured to minimize taxes, you may miss opportunities or adopt a risk profile that is overly conservative.

Example: One investor is saving with the intention of opening his own business in 20 years. He will need $200,000, and he wants his portfolio to average a 10 percent return per year. During the first three years, funds are placed in a growth mutual fund, where the average compounded yield is approximately 22 percent. On an after-tax basis, this is the equivalent of a 14.75 percent return, well above the target net return of 10 percent.

In the interest of diversification, in the fourth year the investor begins placing funds in a tax-deferred account. Here, the average yield is only 7 percent.

As long as funds are equally divided between the two investments, the 10 percent goal will still be met. However, if the investor places a greater portion of the total portfolio in the lower-yielding account, the average return will fall below the 10 percent target.

Do not allow the tax consequences of your investments to rule your decisions. Rather, be aware of taxation as one of several problems to be managed or mitigated by the way you invest. The investor in the previous example can achieve diversification in rate and risk and still meet a long-term goal; too much emphasis on tax savings violates that goal.

The same argument can be applied to excessive emphasis on the rate of return. If you are willing to assume greater risks, you can place funds in higher-yielding investments. If successful, you will certainly meet your goal; but if the market falls, you will fall short as well.

Chapter 2 examines the steps necessary in formulating your plan for success.

CHAPTER 2

The Formula for Success

The minority of investors who consistently beat the odds have one thing in common: They understand clearly what they want to achieve, and they do not vary from the course they set for themselves.

You will succeed as an investor by being aware that the process demands self-discipline. Too many investors do not set specific goals beyond making a profit as quickly as possible, and they forget the importance of establishing personal policies for managing their investment capital. In this chapter, you will see how these steps can be completed *before* money is placed at risk.

Goal-Oriented Investing

People in business—including presidents of companies, managers, and entry-level employees—quickly learn the importance of setting goals. A president may decide to move into a new market this year or to cut expenses by 10 percent. A manager may set a goal of improving efficiency or of changing procedures while reducing the rate of errors. An employee may resolve to master a complicated procedure to improve job skills. These people all have recognized that they are most likely to achieve when they have a target. The more specific that target, the better. Yet the same people who act in a very goal-oriented manner in business might invest their own money in a very haphazard fashion.

The rules that are so regularly practiced in business also apply to investing. The goal itself dictates the appropriate avenue for getting there. A goal that may require liquidity within the next five years should be reached through highly liquid investments. A fund that you cannot afford to lose should be placed in a very safe investment where capital loss risk is minimal. And if your income is higher than average, you will need tax deferral to avoid tax penalties each year.

> *Example:* One family's immediate goal is to set up an emergency reserve fund, money that will be available in case expenses come up beyond the regular budget. The obvious place to deposit this fund is a local bank, a money market fund, or some other place where it will be easily and quickly available. Putting the money in savings bonds or a limited partnership would be inappropriate. That would defeat the purpose of the fund.

> *Example:* A family is beginning to save money for its child's college education. It has 15 years to accumulate an adequate fund. Speculating with the money is not necessary, since the family has many years to save; thus, buying volatile stocks or other high-risk investments is not the best way to achieve this goal. Tax deferral plus regular, compounded growth would be possible through an IRA account or savings bonds.

Many investors are so preoccupied with rates of return and speculative profits that they completely lose sight of their goals—or never set goals at all. The typical stock market investor experiences gains and losses in such equal measure that the average return is lower than what a more conservative savings account would yield. However, the tendency is to chase fast profits, with little regard for other goals.

Another problem is the allure and excitement of risk. Many investors are willing to speculate primarily because the potential exists for big gains in a very short period of time. But there is an equal chance of loss, and there are more losers than winners in the most speculative markets. Just as the gambler is drawn to the longest odds, many market speculators are attracted by the process more than by the idea of reaching a specific goal.

A savings account or mutual fund, admittedly, is far less exciting than some of the more glamorous markets. However, the risk of loss should always be viewed in line with your goals. If you are compelled to gamble, do so with a small portion of your total portfolio. Leave the bulk of your capital in investments appropriate to the goals you have set for yourself.

Goals and Policies

Investors, in an attempt to set goals, may be distracted by the attributes of a particular product. You will find that many investment advisers and salespeople mistake attributes for goals.

A *goal* is a desired end result, the purpose for which you invest in the first place. Your goal, by clarifying the time involved and the purpose of investing, defines the types of investments that are appropriate for you. It also defines, to some degree, the amount of risk you should be willing to assume.

An *attribute* is a feature of an investment. For example, an account may be insured by a federal agency, it may be highly liquid, or it may contain diversification (a mutual fund, for example, diversifies its investment pool among many different investments).

Attributes are often defined as the *profile* of an investment. For example, a mutual fund may describe its profile as "seeking aggressive long-term growth with high current income." This is not a goal; it is an attribute of the product that may or may not fit your goals. However, a salesperson may describe this profile as a goal.

> *Example:* You meet with an investment salesperson and describe your financial condition. After the introductory interview, the salesperson shows you the prospectus of a mutual fund. "This fund meets your goals," she states. "It seeks long-term growth and high current income."

It is easy to lose sight of your goals when responding to statements such as this. You may become convinced that, in fact, those *are* your goals. Ultimately, this distraction makes it easy for a salesperson to convince a client to buy shares of the fund, but it does not address your real concerns.

A *risk profile* also is not a goal. Diversification, for example, is not a goal but a feature of an account that may fit your own risk tolerance level.

> *Example:* You are discussing your investment portfolio with a friend. "What's your goal?" your friend asks. You answer, "Diversification."

> *Example:* You have a clearly understood goal, which is to save money in order to start your own business. To reach that goal, you identify several investments to match your risk profile. That means diversifying and minimizing market risks.

You may, indeed, want to diversify a limited investment portfolio. That is a risk profile issue, however, and not the goal itself.

Once you have made a distinction between investment goals and attributes of products, you will have taken an important step in defining your own formula for success. The next step is to set policies, or rules, for yourself. These rules may include definitions of risks you are willing to take and risks you will not take. They may also define the percentage of your portfolio that will be placed in conservative accounts and the small percentage to be used for more speculative ideas.

The policies you set establish the discipline you are willing to apply to yourself. They not only help you limit risks, manage your portfolio, and stay with a program based on goals; they also provide guidelines for future actions. Of course, the rules you set for yourself are only effective if you are willing to follow them.

> *Example:* An investor bought 100 shares of stock last month. The market value increased 15 percent the first week, and the investor did not sell, hoping the trend would continue. But since then, value has fallen several points below the purchase level. Now, the investor wants to hold until the shares once again move into the profitable range.

In this situation, the investor can never sell. He is not willing to take a loss. When the shares do become profitable, the investor hesitates, hoping even more profit can be earned. When shares are at a loss, the investor hesitates again, hoping value will return. No policy has been established, so the investor has no idea what to do.

If the same investor had set firm policies before buying the stock, a decision would have been automatic.

> *Example:* You purchase 100 shares of stock and set a policy for yourself. You will sell in one of two conditions: when shares are 15 percent higher than the purchase price, or when they are 10 percent lower.

If the investor in the first example had followed this rule, he would have realized a 15 percent profit within a week of purchasing shares; if the stock had fallen in value, losses would have been cut by applying the same rule.

If you invest with longer holding periods in mind, this example—going in and out of holdings—does not apply. But the idea is the same. With a clear goal in mind and with an understanding of how much risk is

---
A C T I O N   C H E C K L I S T

Personal Investing Goals

1. List your short-term goals (one year or less).
2. List your intermediate goals (one to five years) and long-term goals (longer than five years).
3. If a married couple, prepare your lists separately. Then compare.
4. Compare goals with investment attributes and risk profiles, seeking a good match.
5. Set specific investing policies.
6. Enforce your own policies, without exception.

---

acceptable, you assume an investment position. Then your future actions will be determined by the policies you establish.

Example: You own shares in a growth mutual fund account, and you want to retire in 17 years. You apply several policies. First, you will reinvest all dividends and capital gains so that earnings will compound over time. Second, you will deposit the same amount each month, without fail. Third, you will increase the amount of monthly investment each time you receive a salary increase.

In this example, specific policies are set for the investment program. As long as you follow these rules, you will reach the ultimate goal.

Inflation and Taxes

Setting goals and making policies help keep you on the right path. Even so, it might seem that there are an overwhelming number of choices to make in the market. You could probably invest your money in hundreds of different ways; so how do you make the best decisions?

In fact, the choice is very narrow. There are two conflicting forces at work in the selection process. Risk increases as potential yield becomes higher, so there is a limit to how high a yield you will be willing to seek. However, a very conservative investment will yield much less than what you consider acceptable. In the middle—between low-yielding safe investments and high-yielding speculative ones—is a fairly narrow band you may think of as the acceptable range. This band is defined by a moderate yield and an acceptable level of risk.

You cannot eliminate risk entirely in any investment. For example, the most conservative strategy might be to place cash in a safety-deposit box. However, inflation will erode the buying power of that money because it will not earn interest. That is a risk in itself. Thus, some risks must be assumed in order to earn a net profit or even to maintain value on an after-tax and after-inflation basis.

Example: In planning your future, you assume that the average annual inflation rate will be 5 percent. If that is reasonable, you will need to earn more than 5 percent to make a net profit— remembering that buying power is diminished by inflation.

Adding to the problem of inflation (which is discussed more fully in Chapter 3) is the question of income taxes. Inflation and taxes together represent a serious problem. You need to earn a net profit *after* inflation and taxes in order to invest successfully. At the same time, you need to respect the risk tolerance level you have established for yourself.

Example: Your investment portfolio earns an average annual rate of 6 percent. You are taxed at the rate of 33 percent. Inflation for the past year ran at 5 percent. On an after-tax and after-inflation basis, you have lost money.

The numbers prove that this example involves a loss. To compute, first add the interest earned; then subtract the taxes that must be paid on the interest; finally, reduce the after-tax value of the entire account by the rate of inflation. If you deposited $1,000 at the beginning of the year, the calculations would go as follows:

Deposit	$1,000.00
Plus 6% interest	60.00
Less 33% tax	19.80
Value	$1,040.20
Less 5% inflation	52.01
Net value	$ 988.19

The $1,000 investment is worth $988.19 after one year, given the combined effects of taxes and inflation. Over a three-year period, the value continues to decline, even when interest is compounded in the account (see Table 2-1).

This calculation is somewhat complicated by the different ways that the columns must be figured. The 6 percent interest column is based on

TABLE 2-1 Effect of Taxes and Inflation

YEAR	PLUS 6% INTEREST	LESS 33% TAX	VALUE	LESS 5% INFLATION	NET VALUE
			$1,000.00		$1,000.00
1	$60.00	19.80	1,040.20	$52.01	988.19
2	63.60	20.99	1,030.80	51.54	979.26
3	67.42	22.25	1,024.43	51.22	973.21

the *gross* (before taxes) payment in the account (assuming that taxes are paid separately and that the account's gross value is not reduced each year). Thus, the gross calculation for the three years is as follows:

YEAR	PLUS 6% INTEREST	VALUE
		$1,000.00
1	$60.00	1,060.00
2	63.60	1,123.60
3	67.42	1,191.02

The compound interest grows in the account; however, each year's earnings are taxed in this example. So the after-tax amount reflects this reduction in the account's value. The real after-tax earnings rate is 4.02 percent (6 percent less 33 percent taxes). In the account itself, the interest still compounds at the annual rate of 6 percent.

The steps involved in calculating your own net value are shown in the worksheet in Figure 2-1a. Note that interest is based on the gross value of the account (before reduction for taxes), as shown in step B. However, the inflation reduction is based on the real after-tax value of the account. This allows you to calculate the interest that will truly be earned in an account without regard for the tax and inflation consequences taking place on the outside, and to also calculate the real net earnings on the same account.

Example: You have $1,000 on account, earning 6 percent per year. Interest is subject to 33 percent tax, and you assume that inflation is running at 5 percent. On the basis of these assumptions, the net value at the beginning of the second year is $988.19 ($1,000.00 plus $60 in interest, less $19.80 for income taxes, and less $52.01 for inflation). The second year's value can be calculated using the worksheet (see Figure 2-1b).

I	Net value, beginning of year	$ _____
II	Plus: interest earned gross value x _____%	+ _____
III	Less: income taxes _____ % x _____ (II)	− _____
IV	Value I plus II less III	$ _____
V	Less: inflation _____ % x _____ (IV)	− _____
VI	Net value I plus II less III less V	$ _____

FIGURE 2-1a Worksheet: Net Profit or Loss

I	Net value, beginning of year	$ 988.19
II	Plus: interest earned gross value x 6 %	+ 63.60
III	Less: income taxes 33 % x 63.60 (II)	− 20.99
IV	Value I plus II less III	$ 1,030.80
V	Less: inflation 5 % x 1,030.80 (IV)	− 51.54
VI	Net value I plus II less III less V	$ 979.26

FIGURE 2-1b Worksheet: Net Profit or Loss

Calculating Breakeven Interest

The double consequences of inflation and taxes show that, in fact, you cannot simply pick a target rate and hope to earn a real net profit. In the previous example, the after-tax earnings rate of 4.02 percent was below the assumed rate of inflation of 5 percent. In this situation, the real value of the investment will continue to decline.

One possible reaction, upon discovering this problem, is to seek investments yielding substantially higher rates and to move money into them. However, this may violate your risk standards. A moderated response is to locate the band of acceptable risks that at least match the tax and inflation cost. Yet another alternative is to defer taxes to reduce the need for higher yields—assuming that tax-deferred products are available and that they also meet your goals.

To calculate the point at which you will break even after taxes and inflation, you need to first calculate two variables:

1. *The assumed inflation rate.* This is the rate you believe will be in effect in the future. You may base your estimate on the Consumer Price Index published by the U.S. government each month and updated each year, or you may choose a different rate.
2. *The effective tax rate.* This is the rate at which taxable income is actually taxed. It is not a percentage of gross income, but the rate in effect after subtracting deductions and exemptions. Use the IRS tax rate schedules to find this percentage, which is based on the taxable income you reported in the most recent year. If your income will be approximately the same for the current year, you should use the same rate.

Figure 2-2 shows the formula for calculating the *breakeven interest rate,* or the rate you need to maintain the value of your capital

$$B = \frac{I}{100 - T}$$

B = breakeven interest rate
I = inflation rate
T = tax rate

FIGURE 2-2 Formula: Breakeven Interest

after taxes and inflation. The assumed rate of inflation is divided by the percentage remaining after the tax rate is applied (100 less the rate).

Example: You are assuming that inflation this year will average 5 percent. Your most recent tax return shows that you were taxed at the rate of 33 percent:

$$\frac{5\%}{100 - 33\%} = 7.46\%$$

In this case, you will need to earn 7.46 percent in order to break even after reducing the value of your investments for inflation and taxes. This is based on the assumption that inflation does run at the 5 percent rate and that you will be taxed at 33 percent of taxable income.

Table 2-2 shows how various tax rates and inflation rates affect the required breakeven interest point. This table shows how the problem is compounded during times of high inflation. A change from a 5 percent inflation rate to a 7 percent rate increases the required breakeven interest from 7.46 percent to 10.45 percent. If you have compared available investment yields and risks, you know that this is a significant gap in yields. During times of higher inflation, interest yields are supposed to be correspondingly higher; however, even if that is true, it does not always follow that risks remain stable during the same period of change.

TABLE 2-2 Breakeven Interest

Tax Rate	Inflation Rate				
	3%	4%	5%	6%	7%
28%	4.17%	5.56%	6.94%	8.33%	9.72%
29	4.23	5.63	7.04	8.45	9.86
30	4.29	5.71	7.14	8.57	10.00
31	4.35	5.80	7.25	8.70	10.14
32	4.41	5.88	7.35	8.82	10.29
33	4.48	5.97	7.46	8.96	10.45

Reaching Your Goals

Many people, unfortunately, believe they are reaching their investment goals when they are not. Inflation and taxes take their toll and are invisible but very real issues. There is nothing you can do to affect the course of national inflation; however, you can plan your investment strategies with taxes in mind.

> *Example:* You base your projections on an assumed inflation rate of 5 percent; you are taxed at the rate of 33 percent. According to the breakeven interest calculation, you will need to earn 7.46 percent or more. You have isolated two investments that will achieve this within your definition of acceptable risk: U.S. savings bonds (yielding a minimum of 7.50 percent, guaranteed), and a time deposit account offered by a local bank and yielding 7.55 percent.

In this example, the time deposit yield is half a percentage point higher than the minimum guarantee on U.S. savings bonds. Both accounts are guaranteed: the time deposit by federal insurance, and the savings bond by the U.S. government. However, the comparison is not complete with those attributes, for several reasons:

1. The savings bond rate is a *minimum* guarantee. Chances are that actual earnings will be higher during the holding period.
2. Savings bond interest compounds, whereas the time deposit account will have to be reinvested upon maturity to achieve the same effect.
3. Most significantly, the savings bond interest is deferred until the bond is cashed in. Unless the time deposit is made within an IRA or a similar deferred account, interest will be taxed in the year it is earned. With this point in mind, the savings bond is preferable to the time deposit account.

These are the types of comparisons that you need to make when analyzing two or more products. The rate may appear to be greater in one than in the other. However, the true earnings yield must include the tax question. Even though you will be taxed eventually in a deferred account, deferral itself grants you much more control over year-to-year tax liabilities.

The tax question is even more significant in times of very high inflation. You may need to seek deferred income to beat the tax and inflation cost without violating your risk standards.

Example: Inflation is relatively high. You expect next year's rate to run at about 7 percent, and you are taxed at the 33 percent rate. To break even, you will need to earn no less than 10.45 percent.

In this situation, you may be unable to find a product that consistently yields 10.45 percent without also accepting much higher risks. However, if the tax problem is removed from the equation, the problem is reduced. Assuming that your capital will lose 7 percent of its buying power per year, the breakeven rate will be much lower. You will not need to worry about 33 percent of your earnings being paid out for taxes.

You cannot separate the question of risk from the concerns for breaking even after inflation and taxes. The next chapter shows how risk and reward work and how risk can be accurately evaluated.

CHAPTER 3

Risk and Reward

You might be drawn to a particular investment because it is advertised as "risk-free." What that usually means is that, through some device such as insurance or a guarantee, you cannot lose your capital. In reality, though, risk comes in several forms.

The risk of losing money is well understood. You can identify the problem in buying common stock, for example: Market value might decrease. If it does and you sell, you will lose part of your investment.

Investors usually evaluate risk, if at all, *after* they decide on the desired rate of return. For example, an investor might begin with the premise that it is possible to earn 8 percent. He then looks for an investment offering that rate of return with the lowest possible risk. But he does not question his rate of return.

The reality is that the rate of return is more than just a percentage. It also serves as a "risk meter" in many cases. The higher the number, the greater the risk, in one form or another. So a 10 percent return can be said to have a risk factor of 10, compared with a 5 percent return with a risk factor of only 5.

In order to select an investment appropriate for yourself and your risk tolerance, you first need to be aware of three types of risk: market, liquidity, and inflation.

Market Risk

Market risk is the best understood of the three types of risk. You may purchase shares of stock only to see market value fall. This can occur when you buy shares of a single company or shares in a mutual fund.

> *Example:* You purchase 100 shares of stock at the current price of $55 per share. Two months later, the market value is $48. Without considering the transaction charges, you would lose $700 if those shares were sold.

> *Example:* You purchase $1,000 of mutual fund shares. The value per share is $21.45, so you have acquired 46.62 shares. A few months later, the share value is $16.50. Value has declined by $4.95 per share (without considering any income earned and credited to your account).

Market risk is a consideration only under two conditions: when the investment is volatile and you are concerned about short-term market value changes, and when you might need to cash in the investment within the next few months or years.

If you select fundamentally strong products, long-term growth will almost certainly offset any temporary market risk. This is especially the case when you plan to reinvest earnings.

> *Example:* You invest $100 per month in a growth mutual fund. You have instructed the management of the fund to reinvest all interest and dividends as they are earned.

In this example, there are two factors offsetting the short-term market risk. The first is the assumed strength of the fund itself. Over the long term, the value of the fund's portfolio is expected to increase. The second is the fact that earnings will be reinvested, meaning that the investment base is continuously increased and income will be compounded.

If you select investments that are well managed or financially competitive (like the common stock of an industry leader), market risk should be viewed as a short-term problem. And if you plan to hold on to your investment for many years, market risk will not necessarily apply to you.

The solutions to market risk include the following:

1. *Select low-yielding, conservative products.* Avoid volatile, unstable, or financially uncertain choices, recognizing that the poten-

tial for big gains will be matched by a corresponding market risk.

2. *Invest in insured or guaranteed accounts.* Examples include savings products offered by federally insured banks, savings and loans, and credit unions; some insurance products; and debt securities issued by the federal government, which are backed by the full faith and credit of the United States.

3. *Diversify.* Avoid market risk by placing segments of your portfolio in dissimilar investments. For example, if you place all of your money in the stock market, shares might move up or down in more or less the same direction. You can also diversify with a limited amount of capital by purchasing shares in a mutual fund. Although the entire portfolio is then invested in the stock and bond market, diversification among issues provides you with a degree of market risk protection.

Liquidity Risk

Another form of risk that is often ignored or simply forgotten is *liquidity risk.* Once you place your money in an investment, what is involved in getting it back when you want it?

Some investments are very liquid. Passbook savings accounts and shares of money market funds, for example, can be cashed out by simply making a withdrawal or writing out a check. Other investments are liquid after a minimum period of time. For example, savings bonds can be cashed at any time after a six-month holding period.

Another group of investments is very illiquid. This does not mean you cannot get your money, only that there is a cost involved. Examples include some annuity products, which may be cashed out only with a penalty, and time deposits, which may be cashed early with loss of interest. You may also cash out your investment in an individual retirement account (IRA) before retirement age. However, you might be subject to a 10 percent penalty as well as to immediate income tax on the amount withdrawn. Real estate is also illiquid. To get your investment back, you must either sell or apply for a mortgage (which is borrowing against your equity).

One final classification is absolutely illiquid: In other words, there might not be a market for your holdings. Suppose you purchase $5,000 in units of a public limited partnership. The program is set up to exist for 10 years. However, three years later you want your money back. You then discover that there is no secondary market for partnership shares. Your only choice is to either hold the investment until the program is liquidated or sell at a large discount to the general partners.

You can avoid liquidity risk in one of three ways:

1. *Diversify your portfolio.* Be sure that a portion of your investment capital is maintained in a highly liquid account so that you can get it if and when it is needed. Then invest a portion in longer-term but illiquid products that meet your goals and conform to your acceptable level of risk tolerance.
2. *Avoid illiquid products altogether.* You might conclude that there is no need for illiquidity and that it is possible to meet your investment goals entirely in liquid investments.
3. *Limit your illiquid investments.* Limit illiquidity to your own home and your retirement fund, and place the balance of the portfolio in more liquid products. For example, suppose you are buying a home and you also place $2,000 per year in an IRA account. Both of these investments are very illiquid. If they are the extent of your portfolio, then you are accepting a very high level of liquidity risk. You can only get your money out by accepting a tax penalty (on the IRA) or going into debt (on your home). You may also sell your home, but you will then need to reinvest your proceeds somewhere else.

Inflation Risk

If you walk the wrong way on a conveyor belt, you will need to move at a greater speed than the belt; otherwise, you will make no progress or even lose ground. The same is true with investing and inflation. All investors face the problem of *inflation risk.*

> *Example:* A very conservative investor has decided to forego a potentially large rate of return. In the desire to reduce market risk, he accepts a 3 percent interest rate. However, inflation is running at the rate of 5 percent. This investor is losing buying power, meaning that capital is worth less each year that inflation outpaces the return.

Of course, your inflation risk might not be as great as that indicated by the published Consumer Price Index, which includes housing and

transportation costs, among other price measurements. If you are buying a home and your payments are fixed, you escape part of the national
inflation rate; and if you don't buy a new car every year, you avoid, or at
least defer, inflation on the cost of transportation.

You can solve inflation risk in the following ways:

1. *Seek tax deferral in your portfolio.* If tax liability is deferred, inflation
   risk becomes more manageable. You can accept a lower rate of
   return and still achieve progress. Suppose that, with your risk
   tolerance in mind, you have identified several possible investments. The average yield is 6 percent. If that yield is taxable,
   approximately 2 percent will go to income taxes each year. That

---

ACTION CHECKLIST

Risk Evaluation

1. Rate your investments in terms of the following:
   a. Market risk.
   b. Liquidity risk.
   c. Inflation risk.
2. Identify solutions for each type of risk:
   a. *Market risk:*
      1) Select low-yielding products.
      2) Avoid volatility in market value.
      3) Invest in companies with exceptional financial
         strength.
      4) Invest in insured or guaranteed accounts
      5) Diversify your portfolio.
   b. *Liquidity risk:*
      1) Diversify so that a portion of your portfolio is
         liquid.
      2) Avoid illiquid products altogether.
      3) Limit the degree of illiquid investments in your
         portfolio.
   c. *Inflation risk:*
      1) Seek tax deferral in your portfolio.
      2) Diversify products *and* risks.
      3) Attempt to outperform the rate of inflation, but
         only if risks are acceptable.

---

leaves a net return of about 4 percent, *before* inflation. If the rate of inflation exceeds 4 percent, you will lose buying power. The solution is to invest in a tax-deferred environment (such as an IRA) or to select investments with deferral features (such as U.S. savings bonds).

2. *Diversify risks.* One form of diversification involves separation not just by product but also by risk level. For example, you might place part of your money in a very conservative, insured account yielding a relatively low return, another portion in a higher-risk product with the potential for a relatively high rate of return, and the largest, middle portion of the portfolio in medium-risk products. If diversification of risk is combined with tax deferral, the overall portfolio becomes much more manageable.

3. *Offset inflation risk with higher returns.* As long as higher risks are acceptable and match your own risk profile, they will match or exceed the rate of inflation—except in the most extreme situations. The danger is that when you concentrate only on inflation risk, you may situate yourself at intolerable levels of market risk.

Computing the Real Return

Comparisons between investments are complicated by the fact that each product may involve completely different costs. For example, a comparison between a mutual fund and a time deposit must take several factors into account. The fund will charge a management fee and possibly other fees as well. If it is purchased through a salesperson, you may also have to pay a commission, or *load*. In addition, the method of compounding will vary in each product; thus, longer-term and shorter-term returns might differ widely.

Keep these points in mind when determining the real return:

1. *Deduct transaction charges if they apply.* When you buy and sell on a public exchange, the brokerage firm charges a fee. This adds to the purchase price and takes away from the sale price.

2. *Consider the tax cost.* A tax-deferred return will be higher than the same percentage return in a taxable account.

3. *Make a realistic comparison over time, keeping compounding rules in mind.* For example, you may compare direct purchase of a

bond with the alternative of placing money in a bond mutual fund. With direct purchase, you will be paid interest twice a year. To achieve any compounding, you will have to reinvest these payments at or above the interest rate of the bond. In comparison, the earnings in the bond mutual fund can be automatically reinvested and so will produce immediate and continuous compounding.

You might start out with the goal of increasing your capital through investments. After viewing the situation realistically, however—meaning with both inflation and taxes in mind—you might change your mind. It is possible to accumulate value even on a net basis, especially with tax deferral. However, if your risk tolerance level is low, a more appropriate goal might be to simply maintain value.

To maintain value, you must increase your portfolio enough to match the after-inflation and after-tax value of your investments. In other words, to maintain your buying power, you will need an ever-growing dollar amount. In times of high inflation, this defensive strategy might be both prudent and necessary, if only because the alternative involves unacceptably high risks.

Calculating Interest

Any comparison between investments should be based on the interest earned per year. This is not the same as the *nominal* (or stated) *interest rate*. The true annual rate will vary with the method of compounding used.

In calculations of interest, the basic formula involves three elements:

1. *Principal.* This is the amount invested, either as a lump sum at the beginning of a period or as a series of deposits made over time.
2. *Rate.* The interest rate may be an annual percentage, or it may be a monthly, quarterly, or semiannual percentage.
3. *Time.* The longer the holding period, the higher the amount of interest.

The basic formula for calculating interest, as shown in Figure 3-1, involves multiplying the three elements together.

$$I = P \times r \times T$$

I = interest
P = principal
r = interest rate
T = time

FIGURE 3-1 Formula: Interest Calculation

Example: A mutual fund has traditionally returned 12 percent per year. If you place $1,000 in the fund today, and if you assume the traditional rate will be earned for one full year, how much interest will the fund earn in 12 months? In this case, the principal is $1,000, the rate is 12 percent, and the time is one year:

$$I = \$1,000 \times .12 \times 1$$
$$= \$120$$

If this example is extended to a second year, is it fair and accurate to assume that another $120 will be earned? The answer is no, since the 12 percent will be earned on the basis of the beginning value of the *second* year. At the start of the second year, the investment will be worth $1,120 ($1,000 plus $120). The formula will therefore be applied as follows:

$$I = \$1,120 \times .12 \times 1$$
$$= \$134.40$$

This is an example of *annual compounding*. The assumption is made that the historical rate of 12 percent will apply each year and that each year's balance will grow by the interest earned during the previous year.

Annual compounding should be used when an assumed rate is applied. For example, if you are estimating average returns in your financial plans, annual compounding should be used. In situations where a rate is guaranteed (such as through a passbook savings account), other methods of calculating interest are involved: on a monthly, quarterly, or semiannual basis. In these cases, the rate per period (month, quarter, or half-year) is a fractional part of the nominal, or annual, rate. To calculate the *periodic interest rate*, divide the annual rate by the number of periods in the year. The formulas for this process are summarized in Figure 3-2. There are 12 months in the year. So for monthly compounding, the annual rate is divided by 12. And there are four quarters or two semi-

MONTHLY   QUARTERLY   SEMIANNUALLY

$$r = \frac{A}{12}$$ $$r = \frac{A}{4}$$ $$r = \frac{A}{2}$$

r = periodic rate A = annual rate

FIGURE 3-2 Periodic Interest Rates

annual periods in the year, so the periodic rates for these periods are divided by 4 (quarters) or 2 (half-years).

The true annual yield is based on the compounding method used. With *monthly compounding*, the balance at the beginning of each month is multiplied by one-twelfth of the annual rate. The result is an annual rate higher than the stated rate. This is proven in Table 3-1, which illustrates what happens when $1,000 is deposited at the beginning of the year and interest of 8 percent is compounded monthly. The periodic rate is .00667, equal to one-twelfth of 8 percent.

$$\frac{.08}{12} = .00667$$

TABLE 3-1 Monthly Compounding

MONTH	8% INTEREST	BALANCE
		$1,000.00
1	$6.67	1,006.67
2	6.71	1,013.38
3	6.76	1,020.14
4	6.80	1,026.94
5	6.85	1,033.79
6	6.90	1,040.69
7	6.94	1,047.63
8	6.99	1,054.62
9	7.03	1,061.65
10	7.08	1,068.73
11	7.13	1,075.86
12	7.18	1,083.04

TABLE 3-2 Quarterly Compounding

QUARTER	8% INTEREST	BALANCE
		$1,000.00
1	$20.00	1,020.00
2	20.40	1,040.40
3	20.81	1,061.21
4	21.22	1,082.43

TABLE 3-3 Semiannual Compounding

PERIOD	8% INTEREST	BALANCE
		$1,000.00
1	$40.00	1,040.00
2	41.60	1,081.60

The true annual yield based on monthly compounding is not the stated rate of 8 percent but the compound rate of 8.304 percent (indicated by the final figure in Table 3-1).

If the same initial deposit is placed in an account yielding 8 percent *compounded quarterly,* the outcome will be different, as shown in Table 3-2. The annual rate for 8 percent compounded quarterly is not the nominal 8 percent, but 8.243 percent.

If interest is *compounded semiannually,* the outcome will again be different, as shown in Table 3-3. The annual rate in this case is 8.16 percent. Thus the true annual rate is always higher than the stated rate when compounding occurs more than once during the year.

The Future Value of 1

In these examples, the assumption has been that a single deposit was made at the beginning of each year. The calculation of interest based on this assumption produces what is called the *future value of 1* (dollar), or the accumulated value of 1. You can calculate this value without having

$$F = D(1 + r)^n$$

F = future value

D = deposit

r = interest rate

n = number of periods

FIGURE 3-3 Formula: Future Value of 1

to figure each period's interest and principal by using the formula shown in Figure 3-3.

Example: You deposit $1,000 at the beginning of the year. The account returns 8 percent, with compounding done monthly. What will the account be worth at the end of the first year?

$$F = \$1,000 (1 + .00667)^{12}$$
$$= \$1,000 (1.083042)$$
$$= \$1,083.04$$

Compare this calculated total with the total in Table 3-1: It is the same. To perform this calculation on a hand calculator, first add '1' to the periodic interest rate (in this example, .00667). Enter this as the first month's periodic rate. Then, if your calculator performs a repeating "equals" function, depress the "total" button 11 times to produce the factors for months 2 through 12. Otherwise, you will need to reenter the periodic rate as a multiplier for each period. Multiply each monthly factor by the deposit amount.

Example: You deposit $1,000 at the beginning of the year. The account returns 8 percent, with compounding done quarterly. What will the account be worth at the end of the first year?

$$F = \$1,000 (1 + .02)^4$$
$$= \$1,000 (1.082432)$$
$$= \$1,082.43$$

Compare this calculated total with the total in Table 3-2: It is the same. To perform this calculation on a hand calculator, first add '1' to the periodic interest rate (in this example, .02). Enter this as the first quarter's periodic rate. Then depress the "total" button three times to produce the factors for quarters 2 through 4. Multiply that by the deposit amount. Again, if your calculator does not have a repeating "equals" function, you will need to enter each calculation's factor separately.

Example: You deposit $1,000 at the beginning of the year. The account returns 8 percent, with compounding done semiannually. What will the account be worth at the end of the first year?

$$
\begin{aligned}
F &= \$1{,}000\ (1 + .04)^2 \\
&= \$1{,}000\ (1.0816) \\
&= \$1{,}081.60
\end{aligned}
$$

Compare this calculated total with the total in Table 3-3: It is the same. To perform this calculation on a hand calculator, first add '1' to the periodic interest rate (in this example, .04). Enter this as the first half's periodic rate. Then depress the "total" button one additional time to produce the annual factor. Multiply that by the deposit amount.

The Future Value of 1 per Period

In some cases, you will not make a single deposit and allow it to grow at interest; instead, you will make a series of regular deposits. In this situation, compound interest must be calculated differently. The formula for calculating the *future value of 1 per period* (or accumulated value of 1 per period) is shown in Figure 3-4.

Example: You plan to deposit $250 at the end ,of each quarter, or $1,000 per year. Interest will be paid at the annual rate of 8 per-

$$
F = D\left[\frac{(1 + r)^n - 1}{r}\right]
$$

F = future value
D = deposit
r = interest rate
n = number of periods

FIGURE 3-4 Formula: Future Value of 1 per Period

TABLE 3-4 Quarterly Compounding, Series of Deposits

QUARTER	DEPOSIT	8% INTEREST	BALANCE
1	$250.00	$ 0	$ 250.00
2	250.00	5.00	505.00
3	250.00	10.10	765.10
4	250.00	15.30	1,030.40

cent, compounded quarterly. Applying the formula, you get the following:

$$F = \$1{,}000 \left[\frac{(1.02)^4 - 1}{.02} \right]$$

$$= \$1{,}000 \left[\frac{.082432}{.02} \right]$$

$$= \$1{,}030.40$$

The accuracy of this calculation can be established by figuring each quarter's interest. Because the first deposit is made at the end of the quarter, there is no interest for the first period. From that point forward, the quarterly interest is based on the previous balance. This is summarized in Table 3-4.

The same procedure is used for periodic rates other than quarterly. However, rather than multiplying the factor by itself four times, multiply it 12 times (monthly) or two times (semiannually).

The Present Value of 1

You face yet another calculation if you want to accumulate a target amount by the end of a period. Then you must calculate what is called the *present value of 1*. The formula for this process is shown in Figure 3-5.

Example: You want to have $1,000 in your savings account by the end of one year. Interest will be paid at the rate of 8 percent,

$$V = T\left[\frac{1}{(1+r)^n}\right]$$

V = present value
T = target amount
r = interest rate
n = number of periods

FIGURE 3-5 Formula: Present Value of 1

compounded quarterly. How much must be deposited today to create a fund worth $1,000? The formula is applied as follows:

$$V = \$1,000 \quad \left[\frac{1}{(1 + .02)^4}\right]$$

$$= \$1,000 \quad \left[\frac{1}{1.082432}\right]$$

$$= \$1,000 \quad [\ .923846 \ ]$$

$$= \$ \ 923.85$$

To prove that this calculation works, begin with the indicated deposit amount. Calculate periodic interest for each quarter, as shown in Table 3-5.

TABLE 3-5 Present Value, Single Deposit

QUARTER	8% INTEREST	BALANCE
		$ 923.85
1	$18.48	942.33
2	18.84	961.17
3	19.22	980.39
4	19.61	1,000.00

Sinking Fund Payments

Present value does not always apply to a single deposit made at the beginning of the period. In some cases, you will want to make a series of deposits, called *sinking fund payments*, and the formula for this calculation is shown in Figure 3-6. In this case you are calculating the *present value of 1 per period*.

> *Example:* You want to accumulate $1,000 within one year. Interest will be paid at 8 percent, compounded quarterly. How much must be invested at the end of each quarter?

$$V = \$1,000 \left[\frac{1}{[(1 + .02)^4 - 1]/.02} \right]$$

$$= \$1,000 \left[\frac{1}{.082432/.02} \right]$$

$$= \$1,000 \left[\frac{1}{4.1216} \right]$$

$$= \$1,000 \left[.242624 \right]$$

$$= \$ \ 242.62$$

This calculation can be proven by working out the quarterly deposits and interest. Because deposits are made at the end of each period, there is no interest for the first quarter. The detailed calculation is summarized in Table 3-6. (The calculation is two units short of $1,000 due to rounding.) Each quarter's interest is based on the balance in the account as of the end of the previous quarter. The same procedure is applied for any rate of interest and any method of compounding.

Calculating interest, either for future or present value, is not compli-

$$V = T \left[\frac{1}{((1 + r)^n - 1) \div r} \right]$$

V = present value
T = target amount
r = interest rate
n = number of periods

FIGURE 3-6 Formula: Sinking Fund Payments

TABLE 3-6 Present Value, Series of Deposits

QUARTER	DEPOSIT	8% INTEREST	BALANCE
1	$242.62	$ 0	$242.62
2	242.62	4.85	490.09
3	242.62	9.80	742.51
4	242.62	14.85	999.98

cated as long as you keep in mind the distinctions between each of the four methods:

1. Future value of 1—shows the future value of an account when a single deposit is made.
2. Future value of 1 per period—shows the future value of an account when a series of deposits are made.
3. Present value of 1—shows the amount of a single deposit that must be made today to reach a target amount in the future.
4. Present value of 1 per period—shows the amount that must be deposited at the end of each period to reach a target amount in the future.

SECTION TWO

Tax Savings
for Tomorrow

CHAPTER 4

A Built-In Income

Virtually every investor eventually needs to plan for a secure retirement. For many, this is a primary long-term goal. You need to solve the problem of uncertainty, however, with most forms of investment. How can you ensure that the income from accumulated capital will be adequate to support you in later years?

One possible source of retirement funds is an annuity. Annuities offer a combination of two attractive features. First, the money placed into an annuity is allowed to grow free of current taxation. The deferral feature increases the yield over a number of years. Second, once you begin withdrawals, payments are guaranteed, either for life or for a specified amount or number of years.

The Annuity Contract

An *annuity* is a contract between an insurance company and the annuity owner. It is the opposite of life insurance. With a life insurance policy, a benefit is paid to your beneficiaries upon your death. In an annuity contract, a series of payments are made to you for as long as you continue to live.

The *owner* is most often also the *annuitant:* the person who will receive monthly payments after a specified age has been reached. However, owner and annuitant may also be two different people. A company, for example, might own an annuity policy for the benefit of a key employee, or one spouse might own an annuity for a separate annuitant (spouse, parent, or child, for example).

When you purchase an annuity, you make a series of payments over time or one lump-sum payment at the inception of the contract. At some point in the future, usually after age 59½, the insurance company will begin making a series of benefit payments to you. In some cases, the payout period begins immediately. The point at which payouts begin is called *annuitization*.

During the time the insurance company holds the money placed into the contract, it is invested. So the money you give the company is calculated as the present value of future benefits. The money deposited, plus compounded income over the life of the contract, is calculated to fund payouts and to produce a profit for the insurance company—all based on assumptions about investment income and your mortality. The actual amount you will receive will be based on your age today and the time until annuitization, your life expectancy, and the insurance company's expectation of its investment yield. The greater the investment yield expectation, the higher your monthly payments.

The amount of payout also depends on whether the contract is a *life annuity* (with guarantee of payments for the rest of your life) or one with a *period certain* (a guaranteed number of years of payments). In a life annuity, the insurance company assumes the risk that you will outlive your life expectancy; if you do, the company will still continue payments. This insurer's risk is similar to the risk assumed when a life insurance policy is issued. The insured person could pass away at any time; if he or she dies after only paying a few premiums, the company will lose money.

With a period certain contract, the insurance company takes on much less risk. It knows that a contract will involve payments for 20 years, for example. On the basis of the amount of money deposited and the likely rate of return from investment, the company can accurately calculate its profit. Thus, a period certain contract will yield a higher payout than a life annuity. With their combination of tax deferral and guaranteed payments in the future, annuities suit conservative retirement planning well. Of course, you may structure your own portfolio to achieve the same benefit, but there is no guarantee that you will select investments that will perform well enough to provide a secure retirement.

The insurance company's contractual guarantee overcomes a considerable risk: The economic risk associated with a longer-than-expected life. In retirement planning, the annuitant—not the company—takes a similar risk. If the annuitant lives beyond the time period he or she planned for, he or she will use up benefits in the retirement plan, but the annuity benefits continue to be paid.

> *Example:* An individual calculated her retirement plan on the assumption that she would live until the age of 80. At age 60, she began drawing monthly benefits from her IRA account. However, she lived well beyond the assumed age.

The economic risk is evident. After being accustomed to a comfortable retirement lifestyle for 20 years, the retired person was left with nothing but social security. With the chances of health problems and with the continuing need for a place to live, the burden had to be shifted to children or to the government. In either event, economic freedom was lost—even with a lifetime of careful planning. The annuity can overcome this problem.

The Immediate Annuity

Under an *immediate annuity* contract, a single lump sum is given to the insurance company at the inception of the contract. Payouts begin immediately or within one year, and continue for life or until expiration of the period certain. This procedure is summarized in Figure 4-1.

Payouts under the immediate annuity contract may be fixed or variable. With a *fixed annuity,* payments or the payout period are fixed, and the insurance company takes on two primary risks:

1. *Mortality risk.* You might live well beyond your life expectancy, in which case the insurer will be required to continue payments beyond its calculated point of profit.

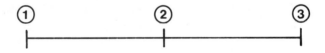

① Lump sum is deposited.

② Proceeds are invested by insurance company and the payout period begins.

③ Life or period certain.

FIGURE 4-1 Immediate Annuity

2. *Interest and expense risk.* There is also the risk that the insurance company will not be able to earn the average rate of investment income it assumes. In that case, the fixed payments must still continue, since they are guaranteed by contract. The company might also experience higher administrative and operating costs in the future, which would affect its profits.

When you buy a fixed annuity, you also assume a risk: that inflation will erode your future purchasing power. What seems adequate today could be far from adequate in a highly inflated economy of the future.

Insurance companies offer a variety of fixed contracts:

1. *Fixed amount annuity.* The contract calls for a guarantee in the amount of monthly payout. The period the contract is to remain in force is calculated on the basis of the amount invested, your age, and the company's investment income assumptions.
2. *Fixed period annuity.* In this contract, the payout period is fixed. The amount of monthly payout varies with the length of the period, your age, and the company's investment income assumptions.
3. *Individual or joint life annuity.* With a life annuity (or pure annuity), a specified level of fixed payments will continue for the rest of your life. Because the insurance company assumes quite a high risk under this contract, the payout amount will be lower than in a more limited benefit contract.

   A variation on the life annuity is the joint and survivor annuity. Under this arrangement, the fixed monthly payment will continue as long as either spouse continues to live.
4. *Individual or joint life and period certain annuity.* Payouts guaranteed for life could continue many decades or a few months. With this problem in mind, an annuity contract may include a provision for a guaranteed amount of total payout, usually for ten or 20 years. If the annuitant dies before that period expires, beneficiaries are entitled to the remaining balance.

   A similar guarantee can be included in a joint and survivor contract. Payouts continue to a surviving spouse for a guaranteed number of years. In the event of death before that period, the balance is paid to beneficiaries.
5. *Individual or joint life and refund certain annuity.* A life and refund certain annuity is similar to the period certain annuity. However, in the event of death, beneficiaries will receive a series of payments until the initial deposit has been refunded. Under the

terms of some contracts, beneficiaries have a choice: either to continue receiving scheduled payments or to accept a discounted lump-sum benefit equal to the present value of future payments. The period certain contract involves time; the refund certain contract involves an amount.

A joint and survivor annuity containing this provision is based on the death of the second spouse.

In the variable annuity, the amount of each payout varies with the company's investment experience. If proceeds are invested to approximate inflation, then buying power should vary according to the rate of inflation.

A variable immediate annuity may be offered in the same varieties as the fixed contract. However, the risks change on both sides. For the insurance company, mortality and expense risk remain; interest rate risk is shifted to the annuitant. However, the annuitant no longer faces inflation risk. Under the variable contract, payments may rise in inflationary times. However, there is also the risk that payments in the future will fall.

The annuitant often is granted a limited range of choices. For example, you could specify that the insurance company is to place your deposits in a mutual fund seeking aggressive growth, moderate growth and income, or high current income. In many instances, deposits can be split among the various products or even transferred from one to another. Mutual funds are the most popular investment vehicle for variable annuities, since the stock market has historically reflected inflationary trends over time.

The Deferred Annuity

Immediate annuities may be appropriate when you have a lump sum to invest. For example, if you are the beneficiary on a life insurance policy and you receive payment, it can be invested so that you will receive a series of payments for the rest of your life. A *deferred annuity*, in comparison, is appropriate for retirement planning over a period of years.

In a deferred annuity contract, the payout date is put off. You may enter a contract and begin making a series of payments over 20 or 30 years, for example, and agree to begin accepting monthly benefits at age 60. The terms of the deferred annuity are summarized in Figure 4-2.

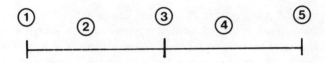

(1)   Contract period begins.

(2)   Deposits are made periodically and are
      invested by insurance company.

(3)   Payouts begin.

(4)   Payout period.

(5)   Life or period certain.

FIGURE 4-2 Deferred Annuity

There are several advantages to the deferred annuity:

1. *Tax deferral.* Earnings are completely tax-deferred until you begin
   making withdrawals. In effect, the compound result with tax
   deferral is greater than it would be if earnings were taxed each
   year.
2. *No annual limit.* You can achieve tax deferral of a similar nature
   with an IRA and also avoid the insurance company's fees for
   setting up the annuity. However, with an IRA, you cannot deposit
   more than $2,000 per year. The deferred annuity has no annual
   deposit limitation.
3. *Guarantees of capital and income.* The capital you deposit under an
   annuity is guaranteed by contract. The terms of payout are also
   guaranteed, either for life (fixed annuity) or according to the company's investment experience (variable annuity).
4. *Planning flexibility.* The retirement planning you undertake today could become obsolete, depending on your changing goals
   and economic status or on changes in inflation. The deferred
   annuity allows you to base the timing of the payout period on
   your individual goals. You can also achieve a tax-free exchange
   by replacing one annuity contract with another. And you can
   defer taxes by converting proceeds from a life insurance policy
   to a deferred annuity contract. (However, you may not de-

fer taxes by moving proceeds from an annuity into a life insurance policy.)

The deferred annuity has one major disadvantage, which is shared by the IRA. If you withdraw funds before age $59\frac{1}{2}$, you will be penalized: You will have to pay taxes on earnings in addition to a 10 percent tax penalty. In addition, the insurance company may charge a fee for early withdrawal, called a *back-end load*. Many contracts specify that this load will apply only for a limited number of years, often on a declining scale. For example, one company might charge 6 percent of all funds withdrawn early, the fee might be reduced by 1 percent per year, and after the sixth year there might be no fee, even for early withdrawals.

Deferred annuities may be purchased with a single premium or through a series of payments. A single premium deferred annuity contract includes a guaranteed rate of interest for an initial period of years. That guarantee is replaced with a new rate later, which may be higher or lower. The contract may also include a minimum guarantee for the entire period. An insurance company often pays a current rate above the guaranteed rate, assuming that its investment experience exceeds estimates.

ACTION CHECKLIST

Annuity Contracts

1. Become familiar with annuities. Determine whether or not they have a place in your portfolio.
2. Study the features of each annuity type.
3. Ask the right questions:
    a. Are annuities appropriate for me?
    b. If so, which type is best for my situation?
    c. What are the risks?
    d. What terms and features do I want and need?
4. Compare annuities with one another in terms of risk features.
5. Compare the cost of annuity contracts by what the insurance company charges you for the risks it assumes.
6. Compare joint life annuity costs with the costs of contracts purchased individually.

A series of deposits may also be made in a deferred annuity contract. If the contract grants you the flexibility to vary payments, you can add to the fund according to your own convenience, a self-determined schedule, or future changes in income.

Taxation of Annuity Benefits

The Tax Reform Act of 1986 included provisions that changed the method of taxation for deferred annuities. Before that legislation went into effect, deferral was generally automatic, regardless of who owned the annuity. However, now only annuities owned by a "natural person" enjoy tax deferral. Thus, a company that owns an annuity for the benefit of an employee cannot defer earnings.

Under the new laws, a portion of the total payout under the contract represents your initial capital, and another portion represents the accumulated earnings. Thus, part of each payout is free from tax (as a return of capital), and part is taxed. The degree of taxable income is determined by applying what is called an *exclusion ratio*. This applies to payments made according to the terms of the contract, but not to early withdrawals.

The ratio is a comparison between the current value of the investment and the expected return. The Internal Revenue Service publishes a series of actuarial tables to be used in determining expected return. The outcome will depend on the type of contract, and the exclusion ratio will vary by age and sex (men and women are subject to different life expectancies). When a contract guarantees a specified total of payments, the exclusion ratio is also affected: The higher the guarantee, the lower the ratio. The formula for the exclusion ratio is shown in Figure 4-3.

> *Example:* An individual has invested $75,000 in an annuity contract over the last decade. Based on contract terms, including age, guarantees, and interest rate assumptions, the expected total re-

$$R = \frac{I}{E}$$

R = exclusion ratio

I = investment total

E = expected return

FIGURE 4-3 Formula: Exclusion Ratio

turn is $100,000. To calculate the exclusion ratio, divide the investment amount by the expected return:

$$\frac{\$\ 75,000}{\$100,000} = 75\%$$

To determine how much of each year's payout will be excluded from income taxes, multiply the exclusion ratio by the amount of payments received:

75% × amount of payments = amount of exclusion

The exclusion ratio determines the percentage of payments free from tax. All payments above that are taxed as current income each year. Once the exclusion amount is completely used up, all future payments are fully taxed. In this example, the entire amount excluded from taxes would be $75,000 ($100,000 × 75%). Anything in addition to that amount would be fully taxed.

The Tax Reform Act of 1986 also changed the manner in which early withdrawals are taxed. If money was invested by August 14, 1982, withdrawals from an annuity are considered first as principal, then as income. This is called the FIFO (first-in, first-out) method. Funds invested after August 14, 1982 are treated first as income, then as principal. This is the LIFO (last-in, first-out) method.

Example: An individual has owned an annuity contract since 1975. In 1991, she makes a partial withdrawal. This is considered a return of her own capital and is not taxed.

Example: Another annuity owner began making deposits in 1984. In 1991, he makes a partial withdrawal. The entire amount withdrawn is treated as current income, to the extent of earnings in the account. Withdrawals above the amount earned level are then treated as return of capital.

The 1986 act also states that if an annuity is pledged as collateral for a loan, current taxes will be due on the amount pledged, up to a maximum of the earnings that have accumulated to that point.

Before 1986, the early withdrawal penalty on deferred annuities was 5 percent. The 1986 act increased it to 10 percent. The penalty applies to withdrawals made before age $59\frac{1}{2}$, but it is waived in cases of death or disability. Penalties can also be avoided if withdrawals are made in a series of payments based on the annuitant's life expectancy. These provisions have changed the rules on annuities so that they are similar to restrictions on IRAs and other retirement accounts. Many annuity benefits were not drastically changed by the 1986 act. Tax deferral is still a viable strategy. For example, a *qualified annuity* is one in which deposits are made on a tax-deferred basis, either by the annuitant or by an employer. In this situation, all proceeds will be taxed upon withdrawal, but all money is protected from tax until that time.

> *Example:* You purchase an annuity contract through your individual retirement account (IRA). You deduct the full $2,000 per year from your gross income, deferring tax on this amount. When you begin withdrawals, all proceeds will be taxed.

> *Example:* An employer makes contributions in behalf of qualified employees and sets up annuity contracts. Employees deposit a portion of their gross pay into the account, and the company makes a matching contribution. The amount the employee pays in is not taxed, since it is not received by the employee as salary. However, when annuitization takes place, *all* proceeds are considered taxable.

Depending on your current tax bracket, sheltering part of your gross income in a deferred annuity could produce a considerable yield just from compounding   not to mention the benefit of having an employer add additional funds for you.

> *Example:* In one company, the benefit plan allows employees to put up to 5 percent of gross income into a deferred annuity account. The employer will add an amount equal to one-half of all funds placed into the retirement account. You earn $50,000 per year and are taxed at the rate of 33 percent. Full participation in the program produces the following result each year:

Contribution, 5%	$2,500
Less tax savings, 33%	825
After-tax cost	$1,675
Plus employer's contribution	1,250
Total benefit value	$2,925

Another way to look at this arrangement is by first-year return on the investment. A deposit of $2,500 "earns" 33 percent just in tax savings.

In the years this money is left on deposit, future earnings will be deferred. In addition, the employer places additional money in your behalf, again increasing not only the investment basis but the deferred benefit as well.

Shopping for Annuities

All annuities are not the same. What might seem very comparable at first glance could be quite different in terms of cost and, ultimately, benefits to you or to your beneficiaries. In shopping for annuity products, compare these features:

1. *The financial history and current financial strength of the company.* Insurance companies have traditionally offered safety and protection, both to insurance policyholders and to annuity contract owners. However, because the annuity is such a long-term contract, the financial strength and stability of the company should be reviewed and compared.
2. *Current and guaranteed interest rates.* Compare current interest rates being paid on fixed-dollar contracts, as well as the period the guarantee lasts. Also find out whether a minimum guarantee rate is offered after the initial guarantee expiration.
3. *Withdrawal terms and privileges.* Find out whether the contract includes a bail-out provision, a clause allowing you to surrender the contract without penalties. What conditions apply, how long does the period last, and what costs would be involved? Are you allowed a free withdrawal privilege? If so, how much (or what percentage) can you withdraw without penalty, and how frequently can such withdrawals be made?
4. *Fees and charges.* Your annuity contract might include a number of different fees and charges. You might be required to pay a *front-end sales load*, which compensates a salesperson by way of commission. In addition, there is probably an annual administration fee. And if you withdraw money, you may also be assessed a back-end load. It may be set for a period of years, last indefinitely, or be scheduled on a declining percentage.
5. *Death provisions.* How will the contract change in the event of your death? Does the contract guarantee that, at the least, your beneficiaries will receive the amount you deposited to that point? If annuitization has begun, how will payments continue?

Will beneficiaries have a choice between continued periodic
payments or lump-sum settlement? What other options will be
offered?

The research you perform before making a decision will determine
whether you find the annuity best suited and priced for your long-term
goals. You should consider an annuity not just as a retirement vehicle
but also as an investment. And the information you gather about the
products offered by competing companies—including both benefits and
restrictions—will determine how much of a bargain you will find in the
market. By becoming informed, you will also be able to decide whether
annuities belong in your portfolio and whether the long-term aspects to
these products are appropriate for you.

Insurance companies offer a range of insurance products in addition
to annuities. In many instances, you can diversify your portfolio and
protect yourself and your family by investing in insurance. The next
chapter discusses these options.

CHAPTER 5

Not Just Life Insurance

You are your family's primary breadwinner. Part of your income goes into investments each year, you are beating inflation, and your future looks secure. Then, without warning and in your highest earning years, you are in a fatal accident.

As unpleasant an idea as this is, such events can occur. Even though this will happen to only a small percentage of families, the point is that it *can* happen.

Life insurance might be the one overlooked aspect of your plan. All the investment planning you do might be worth nothing if long-term plans are drastically changed because your family's income stream stops suddenly. The purpose of life insurance is to provide for your beneficiaries in the event of your unexpected, premature death.

Life Insurance in Your Plan

The value of insuring against an unlikely event is often misunderstood, even by the most sophisticated investors. Insurance is necessary in any situation where your unexpected death would create an economic hardship for your survivors. If your spouse and children depend on your income, if you have mortgage payments each month, and if you are saving money for a secure retirement, you probably need to protect your family and your plan with insurance.

Death is a certain event, but its timing is uncertain. This obvious but important point tells you that, unless your family does not depend on you for support, your plan should allow for such an uncertainty. Many types of insurance protect you against losses that might never happen.

Example: You are purchasing a home, and you pay annual premiums on a fire insurance policy. The chances that your home will be lost in a catastrophe are slim. However, if it were to happen, you could not afford the loss.

Any contingency that cannot be known in advance but that would create an economic loss can be covered by insurance. That includes unlikely events such as fire, theft, and liability, as well as the certain event of death, the timing of which is impossible to know in advance.

Some people confuse insurance with wagering. In a wager, someone who would benefit from your death might put up money on that basis; however, he or she does not have a prior economic stake in your life. A beneficiary in a life insurance policy, however, has an *insurable interest*, meaning that, in the event of a loss, he or she would suffer economically. The premature death of the family's primary earner is an example.

Insurance companies offer protection to a large number of people and collect premiums over a period of years. Some of the people covered by contracts might die a week after making their first premium payment, and others will live for many decades. Overall, though, the premium levels are calculated to pay the death claims that do arise, as well as the insurance company's expenses. The risk is spread among all of the people buying each type of policy.

This risk spreading applies to all forms of insurance. Both the insurance company and each person who owns a policy share in the risks.

Example: Only a small number of residences will have fires this year. Thousands of homeowners pay the premium on homeowner's insurance, even though they know they will probably not suffer a loss. With the total of premiums collected, the insurance company has calculated that it will be able to afford to pay all claims, cover its expenses, and make a profit. All those who are covered by insurance know that in the unlikely event of a fire they will be reimbursed for their loss.

A homeowner has an insurable interest in his or her home, because of the economic stake. Your beneficiaries have a similar interest in your life.

Your long-term plans are invariably based on the assumption that you will be alive by the deadline. A child's college education, retirement, buying or paying off a home, starting a new business—all popular long-term goals—will be realized if you plan and save, but only if you are still alive by the deadline. These goals will be changed in the event of your untimely death. For this reason, a complete financial plan cannot be limited to the use of money that is available to invest. One difficulty in finding an affordable and adequate insurance policy is in having to deal with an agent, whose income is based on commissions. So you cannot know whether you are getting the best policy for your circumstances without doing a little research yourself. Today, insurance is not necessarily just protection. Many products have been developed that combine insurance with investment features.

Term Life Insurance

Before considering insurance products with flexible investment features, it is best to compare the traditional alternatives: term and whole life.

Term insurance provides only one benefit: In the event of the insured person's death, the beneficiary will receive the *face amount* of the policy (the amount of protection promised upon maturity). The only value of term insurance is the protection it provides against your unexpected and untimely death. *Whole life insurance* is a variation in which cash value— the savings component—is built up over a number of years. When cash value is equal to the face amount of the policy, you may withdraw the entire amount—to use for retirement, for example. Whole life insurance is discussed further in the next part of this chapter.

Term insurance is the cheapest kind to buy, and it is the best bargain if you only want insurance. You might want to manage your investment portfolio on your own and take care of your insurance needs as economically as possible. However, term insurance also yields the lowest commission scale for salespeople, so they are motivated to sell you other forms of insurance, which yield greater profits for the insurance company as well as higher income for themselves. Even the most concerned, ethical insurance agents will be unable to ignore the reality: They will earn a better living by selling you a different policy.

This problem has created a long-standing debate in the financial community. One side believes in the idea "Buy term and invest the difference." The other side states that, realistically, most people will not invest the difference, so insurance should be used to build a tax-deferred lump sum to be used for retirement.

There are two types of term insurance: level term and decreasing term. A *level term policy* offers a steady face amount, but your premiums rise periodically. As your age increases, the likelihood of death increases as well. The mortality factor dictates that level term insurance will become more expensive as you age. *Decreasing term* is one alternative. Premiums remain steady as long as you keep the policy in force; however, the face amount of the policy declines each year.

Which of these policies is appropriate will depend on your circumstances. As your investment portfolio grows over a number of years, the economic need for insurance might decrease. If your children grow up and leave home, the risk of economic loss is diminished, since fewer people will depend on you for continuing support. In both these situations, decreasing term would be appropriate.

On the other hand, a level term policy might be the best buy while your children are living at home, while you owe money on a home mortgage, and while your career is still developing.

> *Example:* One family recently purchased its first home and is committed to 30 years of mortgage payments. It is also expecting a second child and is putting money away each month for college education years later. For the next 20 years, the need for insurance will be constant.

Considering the long-term nature of financial commitment in this case, level term is probably most appropriate. The family is committed to 30 years of mortgage payments and at least 20 years of child-raising expenses, to then be followed by the cost of a college education.

Again, in other circumstances, decreasing term insurance might provide all the protection you need. If you have two incomes, for example, insurance can be used only to protect against the economic hardship connected with existing debts.

> *Example:* Both spouses have careers, and their combined income is necessary to afford the high mortgage payments on their home. If the mortgage were not a factor, the family could survive on either salary. They purchased a decreasing term life insurance policy on both lives. In the event of either spouse's death, insurance proceeds would enable the survivor to pay off the mortgage.

In this example, the economic risk of an unexpected death is offset by a decreasing term policy. The face amount will decline each year, but so will the mortgage. In later years, when the face amount is relatively low but the premiums continue at the same level, it might be possible to convert to a level term policy, or even to replace the policy or cancel altogether. For now, the risk has been offset through the right kind of insurance.

Whole Life Insurance

Term insurance is inexpensive compared with whole life because the insurance portion of whole life is only part of the cost. In whole life, you are also paying for the accumulated cash value that builds over the years.

The yield on a whole life policy is traditionally very low—2 or 3 percent per year. That does not keep up with inflation, but it *is* a forced savings account. Another feature of whole life insurance that has made it attractive in the past is the policy loan: You are allowed to borrow your cash value at a very low rate of interest. A policy loan reduces the death benefit by the same amount until it is paid back. Today, however, policy loans are less attractive than in the past because interest can no longer be deducted on your income tax return (except when proceeds are used to invest, in which case interest can be deducted to the extent of investment income).

With a whole life policy, you enjoy the face value protection as well as a growing cash value. This idea is illustrated in Figure 5-1. The time involved is the policy period to a specified age (often age 65). The annual premium is paid for insurance, and cash value builds on the basis of compound interest throughout the policy term. Thus, it builds very

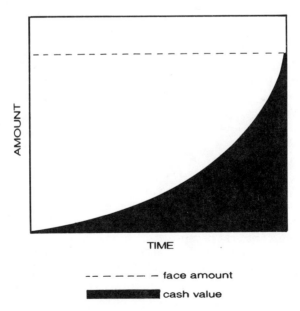

FIGURE 5-1 Whole Life Insurance

slowly in the early years and accelerates later on. The curve in Figure 5-1 is similar to the that for a savings rate in an account paying compound interest.

Some whole life policies also pay a dividend which is a partial return of premium. These are called *participating policies*. A quarterly or annual dividend is declared and paid to each policyowner. The amount of the dividend is based on the company's profit or loss experience. The greater its profits from whole life policy business and from its own investments, the higher the declared dividend. This payment is usually tax-free because it is considered a return of premium rather than income.

Dividends may be used in a number of ways. You can instruct the insurance company to apply dividends to your next premium, to hold the dividends and invest them to produce future income, or to purchase additional insurance.

Because whole life policy yields are extremely low when compared with those of other investments, the insurance industry has undergone drastic changes. The old argument that people who buy term insurance will not invest the amount they save does not work. As consumers became more aware of their choices during the 1970s and 1980s, insurance companies were forced to make their policies more attractive to the comparison shopper in the market.

The movement away from traditional marketing led to the development of a series of products that offer much more than protection and token investment value. In these products, the payment made by the policyowner includes an insurance premium *and* investment capital. The company acts as money manager for the policyowner, but the policyowner takes on the investment risk or accepts a guaranteed rate of return, a choice many people are willing to make for a more acceptable yield over the long term. These products include variable life and universal life insurance.

Variable Life Insurance

In 1976, insurance companies began offering a new form of product: *variable life insurance*. Variable life guarantees some benefits while also allowing the insured to take on some investment risk with the savings portion of the contract. Because it includes investment features, this product must be registered as a security with the Securities and Exchange Commission (SEC). That also means that an individual with only an insurance license cannot sell the product. The salesperson must pass an examination given by the SEC before he or she may offer variable life insurance products.

The plan includes a death benefit that is guaranteed at a minimum level. No matter how poorly the investment side turns out, that guarantee cannot be reduced as long as the policyowner continues making premium payments each year. Because the guarantee is part of the contract, the insurance company continues to assume its mortality risk and its expense risk, as it would with a whole life or term insurance policy. The mortality risk arises from the possibility that any policyholder could die at any time, even before premiums adequate to pay the claim were collected. And because the insurance premium will not change, the insurance company also takes a risk that its future expenses will be higher than the levels calculated when the policy was sold.

Unlike with whole life insurance, however, with variable life the policyholder takes on the investment risk. This policy is therefore appropriate for those who prefer investing in stocks and bonds or short-term interest products rather than in the more conservative long-term investments made by insurance companies. Variable life policyowners are allowed to direct their own investments by selecting one or more mutual funds or other accounts. They then direct the company to place their funds in the accounts of their choice, where all earnings accumulate on a tax-deferred basis.

Variable life directly addresses the criticism of whole life. With this product, the company invests money as you instruct while also guaranteeing a minimum death benefit. If your investments do well, you will beat the traditional whole life rates.

Variable life seems to be a worthwhile combination of insurance and investment goals, with the tax-deferral feature added in. However, the company also assesses annual charges, and it may also penalize you if you cancel the policy and withdraw your funds. You have less investment flexibility with this product than you would have by purchasing a term policy and then investing separately, assuming you would be able to achieve tax deferral in the same manner.

The consumer's response to variable life has been positive. Since its introduction, this product has increased in popularity at the expense of whole life. Perhaps the one factor preventing it from catching on to a greater extent is the regulatory problem. Anyone selling variable life must be a registered representative under the jurisdiction of the SEC. A good number of insurance professionals cannot offer variable products for this reason, even in today's environment, where consumers expect their advisers to be versatile and capable of offering a range of choices.

Obviously, a primary advantage in variable life is the freedom to direct your own investments. But this is also a primary risk. If your timing is wrong, the investment side of the package may lose money. If you fail to diversify, the downside risk could deplete the value of your account, at least temporarily. But variable life insurance does enable you to direct your own portfolio and to possibly improve on traditional whole life returns.

Universal Life Insurance

Once variable life products had been on the market for a few years, the insurance industry recognized the limitations in the product. The need to register salespeople with the SEC, plus the uncertainty of investment performance, excluded a large portion of the insurance market. Buyers of insurance are generally more cautious and conservative than the average person, and the most attractive feature of variable products was, for some, the one factor that kept many people away: having to assume investment risk.

In 1979, another conduit product was developed and offered to the public. *Universal life insurance* expands on the concept of insurance-plus-investment with competitive rates of return. First, it offers a degree of safety on the investment side. A current investment rate is guaranteed each year, and a new rate is announced annually. Second, part of the total premium goes into insurance, and that part may be raised or lowered periodically. Another part is invested.

Flexibility on the insurance side makes universal life a good planning tool. You may need to increase or decrease the amount of life insurance in force, depending on changing economic conditions and your personal goals.

> *Example:* The primary earner in one family owned a universal life insurance policy. When the family added another child, it decided to increase its life insurance coverage. If it had owned a whole life or term policy, it would have had to purchase an additional insurance policy; under the terms of the universal life contract, the family was allowed to modify the existing level of protection.

> *Example:* An individual was making premium payments on a universal life insurance policy for several years. Then a child left home and began a career. The family's insurance needs were lower, so it instructed the company to reduce the amount in force.

There are, of course, several drawbacks. If you want to increase the coverage within a universal life policy, you might be restricted to certain limitations. The company may require additional evidence of insurability, which may mean filling out an application or submitting proof of a medical examination. There may also be a ceiling on the amount of additional insurance you will be allowed to add. Finally, the cost of having a universal life policy might not be evident at the beginning. Some companies will charge a load fee for making changes or for cancellation, as well as annual administration fees and charges.

On the investment side, the appeal of universal life is in the rate guarantee. However, this is a limited benefit. The guarantee is given for only one year, and you have no control over the rate promised next year, or in five or ten years. The percentage will vary depending on how profitably the insurance company is able to operate in the future. The guaranteed rate will be conservative enough so that the insurance company's risks are minimal. The actual rate paid may be above the guaranteed rate.

For the insurance company, the expense and mortality risk remain. For the policyowner, the freedom to control the investment side is given up in exchange for the perpetual guarantee; however, the risk is that future guarantees and actual yields will be lower than what you will need and want. If the insurance company's own experience is poor, the return might not beat inflation.

Universal Variable Life Insurance

Both of the original conduit products addressed special concerns and demands for the consumer. However, they also contained restrictions. In 1985, a new product emerged that combined the attractive features of both: *universal variable life insurance.*

The flexibility to change the insurance face amount and premium level (in universal life) and the freedom to control the investment portfolio (in variable life) give this product its market appeal. The policyowner controls the entire insurance and investment package, and the company acts both as insurer and as money manager.

With this kind of insurance, you are free to direct your investments through a series of mutual funds, interest-bearing accounts, mortgage pools, and other product choices. Interest, dividends, and capital gains in the accounts are not taxed but are treated as deferred income. The most desirable result of owning a universal variable life policy is that investment returns might be high enough each year to pay for the insurance premium. If so, you will not need to put additional money into the product each year to keep the insurance in force. At the same time, the investment value will continue to grow with no current taxes.

In one sense, this is a very attractive feature. It is contingent, however, upon achieving a high enough return on investment to pay premiums. The insurance cost—whether paid in cash or from investment returns—may still be higher than in a basic term insurance policy. This point may be overlooked at the time a salesperson is selling the idea to you. The salesperson will emphasize that your insurance will be "free." In reality, you never have free insurance. Your investment income is simply being used to fund insurance rather than being left to grow at compound rates over time.

Even though universal variable life is an appealing and convenient method for protecting against the economic loss associated with premature death, it might not be the best buy. The problem with any creative variation on insurance protection is in the cost of the insurance itself. Whenever you are comparing the cost of policies, remember this point: You can protect your beneficiaries with life insurance in many forms. Do

ACTION CHECKLIST

Life Insurance

1. Review your life insurance needs and coverage now, and repeat at least once a year.
2. Coordinate life insurance protection with other elements of your plan.
3. For simple insurance protection, do not overlook term coverage.
4. Review features, benefits, and limitations of each type of insurance:
    a. Level Term.
    b. Decreasing term.
    c. Whole life.
    d. Variable life.
    e. Universal life.
    f. Universal variable life.
5. Evaluate the investment value of variable and universal life intelligently:
    a. Compare investment value to value of other investments.
    b. Compare insurance costs to costs of other insurance plans.
    c. Consider the relative cost and benefit terms of separate insurance and investment programs.

not overlook the cost factor on the insurance side or allow yourself to be distracted by the flexibility on the investment side.

For many investors, the tax deferral and convenience of conduit policies offset the costs. However, you will always enjoy greater flexibility by controlling your own investment portfolio, whether on your own or through a universal variable life policy. An insurance policy should be bought because adequate protection is offered at an affordable price. And to determine what this price is, remember to compare back-end loads and other fees charged by the insurance company.

You should also be aware that the Tax Reform Act of 1986 modified some of the rules concerning withdrawals from conduit insurance accounts. Tax deferral may be reduced when the value on the investment side changes. And a portion of a death benefit paid to a beneficiary could be taxed because of the mixture of investment and insurance features.

Again, it is a mistake to purchase a policy only because the company offers flexibility on the investment side or only because taxes are deferred on income. If your primary interest is in tax deferral, you should shop for a basic term insurance policy and keep investments separate. The next chapter shows how flexible, tax-deferred investing is achieved through a number of retirement accounts. You may conclude that you do not need to combine insurance and investing just to defer your tax liability.

CHAPTER 6

Investing Through Your IRA

Investments are often compared and judged solely on the basis of taxability. A municipal bond might be preferred over common stocks because interest is not taxed, for example. When you invest through an individual retirement account, or IRA, you can place funds in products that are normally taxed and defer tax liabilities at the same time.

You might have heard that the IRA is dead, now that contributions cannot always be deducted from adjusted gross income. In fact, though, the IRA continues to offer one of the most convenient methods for investing in a wide range of products while enabling you to defer taxes at the same time.

Before 1982 IRAs were available only to people who did not participate in any other qualified plan. The term *qualified* refers to deferral of taxes and compliance of a plan's terms with the rules allowing that tax status. So if your employer made contributions each year to a retirement plan in your behalf, you could not open and fund an IRA under the pre-1982 rules.

The Economic Recovery Tax Act of 1981 (ERTA) introduced sweeping changes in many areas, including the tax treatment and availability of the individual retirement account. Beginning in 1982, anyone could place up to $2,000 per year in an IRA. The entire amount could be excluded from tax, and all earnings in the IRA were free from tax until withdrawn. From the moment the new law went into effect, IRAs were a success.

The picture changed again when the Tax Reform Act of 1986 was passed. Under the modified rules, the deductibility of IRA contributions was restricted. Some people are still allowed the full amount, but others can reduce only part of their adjusted gross income. Many people have lost the deductibility altogether.

IRA Rules

Even if you cannot deduct contributions to an IRA, IRAs are still valuable because all earnings in your account will be tax-deferred until withdrawals begin. This is the primary benefit of the IRA. If you need and want tax deferral, the IRA gives you great flexibility in diversifying your account without worrying about the tax consequence of profits.

Here are the rules for IRA accounts:

1. *Opening the account.* Your IRA account can be opened for any year by the tax-filing deadline for that year. For example, you may decide to begin IRA investing in 1991. You have until April 15, 1992 to open the account and place up to $2,000 in it.

2. *Contribution level.* You are allowed to contribute $2,000 or 100 percent of your earned income each year, whichever is less. For example. if your earned income last year was only $1,500, that would be the maximum you could contribute to an IRA. When earned income (salaries, self-employment income, and so forth) is greater than $2,000, you can contribute the maximum of $2,000.

   There is no minimum. If you want to put in less than the allowed amount, you have the right to do so.

   The maximum is raised to $2,250 if your spouse has no compensation. You will then have two accounts, your own IRA and the spousal IRA. The total of $2,250 can be split in any way you want between the two accounts.

3. *Early withdrawal penalties.* The purpose of the IRA is long-term savings and tax deferral. Later sections in this chapter will explain withdrawal rules and exceptions in more detail. For now, keep in mind this general rule: If you withdraw funds from your IRA before you reach age $59\frac{1}{2}$, you will be taxed on the amount withdrawn; in addition, you will have to pay a 10 percent tax penalty on all amounts withdrawn.

4. *Withdrawal schedule.* You are allowed to begin withdrawing money from your IRA without penalty at any time after you have reached age $59\frac{1}{2}$. Withdrawals *must* begin by age $70\frac{1}{2}$. The mini-

mum you are required to take by that age is based on your life expectancy.

An exception to the withdrawal schedule is allowed in case of death or disability. Your beneficiary may begin withdrawals without penalty if you die before the minimum age, and you also avoid the withdrawal penalty in the event of total disability. In either case, the tax-deferred portion of the IRA will be taxed as ordinary income in the year withdrawals are taken.

You can also begin early withdrawals at any time if the amounts you take are approximately equal and are based on your life expectancy. This will be explained in more detail later in the chapter.

5. *Deductibility of contributions.* If you and your spouse do not participate in any other qualified plan, you are allowed to deduct the full $2,000 per year contributed to an IRA, without limitation. If only one spouse participates, this privilege is amended.

A single person who participates in another plan may not be allowed the full deduction. The same rule applies to married couples, even when only one spouse is a plan participant.

The Limited Deduction Rule

If you are participating in another qualified plan (such as a retirement plan offered by your employer), the deductibility of IRA contributions depends on your adjusted gross income (AGI), which is your income less allowable deductions before itemized deductions and tax exemptions are taken. For purposes of this computation, adjusted gross is calculated before including the IRA contribution. However, the true AGI on your tax return will be reduced by the amount of allowable IRA contributions.

> *Example:* Your adjusted gross income is $46,000, without including an $800 allowable IRA deduction. On your tax return, the reported AGI is $45,200, which includes the deductible IRA contribution.

Table 6-1 summarizes the ranges of income in which full or partial deductions are allowed and the limits above which no deduction is

TABLE 6-1 IRA Deductibility

	FULL DEDUCTION	REDUCED DEDUCTION	NO DEDUCTION
Single	up to $25,000	$25,001–$35,000	over $35,000
Married, filing joint return	up to $40,000	$40,001–$50,000	over $50,000
Married, filing separate return	not available	$0–$10,000	over $10,000

allowed. The deductible portion of the total possible $2,000 is calculated in the following steps:

Step A: Subtract the deductible limit (Table 6-1) from adjusted gross income.
Step B: Divide the result of step A by $10,000.
Step C: Multiply the result of step B by $2,000. This is the excluded amount.
Step D: Subtract the answer to step C from $2,000. This is the amount you are allowed to deduct on this year's tax return.

Example: A married couple is filing a joint return showing adjusted gross income of $46,000 (before allowing for deductible IRA contributions). The couple's income is between $40,000 and $50,000, so the amount above the full deduction limit is $6,000:

Adjusted gross income	$46,000
Full deduction limit	40,000
Amount above limit	$ 6,000

This amount is divided by $10,000, and the result is then multiplied by the maximum of $2,000:

$$\frac{\$6,000}{\$10,000} \times \$2,000 = \$1,200$$

The final step is to deduct this total from the maximum per year, or $2,000:

Maximum allowed per year	$2,000
Less nondeductible amount	1,200
Deductible portion	$ 800

This family is allowed a deduction of $800 this year. The full $2,000 may still be contributed, but adjusted gross income cannot be reduced beyond the maximum of $800.

A similar calculation is performed for a single person but using a different schedule.

Example: A single person has adjusted gross income (without including IRA deduction) of $32,650 this year. The full deduction level in this instance is $25,000 (see Table 6-1). The calculation of the nondeductible portion begins by isolating the amount about that level: $32,650 less $25,000 is $7,650. The nondeductible portion is calculated as follows:

$$\frac{\$7,650}{\$10,000} \times \$2,000 = \$1,530$$

When this amount is subtracted from the maximum of $2,000 per year, the result is $470. This is the amount by which AGI can be reduced. Again, the single person may contribute less than this amount, or more, up to the maximum of $2,000. But only $470 is free from tax.

The question of deductibility is significant in the year a tax return is filed. In one respect, it represents an immediate return on the investment. However, from that point forward, the real benefit—annual deferral of all taxes on earnings—becomes much more important.

Example: You are in the highest tax bracket this year, and you will have to pay 33 percent of your last dollars earned in federal income taxes. This "taxable" income rate does not apply to the entire amount of income. However, that rate does mean that any reduction of taxable income will result in an immediate savings equal to 33 percent.

If you are allowed a full deduction of $2,000 in IRA contributions for the year, the savings equal $660 (33 percent of $2,000). This is a significant saving, achieved through reduced tax liability.

Withdrawals of IRA Money

When you have reached age $59\frac{1}{2}$ and before you are $70\frac{1}{2}$, you have maximum flexibility. You can withdraw as much or as little as you want, and you are taxed only on the taxable portions withdrawn, which include the following:

1. All contributions made in the past and deducted from adjusted gross income.
2. All accumulated earnings in the account.

There is no tax on amounts contributed to the IRA but *not* deducted from adjusted gross income. This raises an interesting planning point: You may be eligible for reduction of adjusted gross income for your IRA contribution, but you may also elect to not claim it.

> *Example:* During the current tax year, your income is relatively small. You are in a low tax bracket, but you expect your income to rise in future years. The IRA is appealing primarily for its long-term tax deferral, but you do not need the current-year deduction. Even though you are qualified to claim a reduction of adjusted gross income, you elect not to. When you do begin withdrawals years later, a higher portion of the account will therefore be exempt from taxation. All earnings and deducted contributions will be taxed as withdrawn.

If you take an early withdrawal, a portion of the total will be subject to tax and the 10 percent penalty. Any amounts contributed but not used to reduce AGI will be exempt from both. An exception is that if you begin withdrawals in "substantially equal installments," even before reaching age $59\frac{1}{2}$, you will not be charged the 10 percent penalty. Some additional rules for this provision are as follows:

1. Scheduled withdrawals must occur at least once per year.
2. Withdrawals must continue for five years or age $59\frac{1}{2}$, whichever is later.
3. The actual amount of the withdrawal will change each year, because of two factors. First, your life expectancy will be changed, so the calculation will have to be modified accordingly. Second, the value of the IRA will be reduced by the amount of previous withdrawals and then increased by any earnings during the year.

Once you reach age $70\frac{1}{2}$, the rules become restrictive. Starting on April 1 of the year after you reach that age, you must begin to withdraw money from your account. The annual amount is based on your life expectancy or on the life expectancies of yourself and your spouse, jointly. The Internal Revenue Service tables are set up to help you compute this. The IRS life expectancy tables can be obtained by writing or calling your local IRS office and asking for free copies of Publication 590 (IRAs) and Publication 575 (pensions and annuity incomes). Each year's withdrawal must be made by December 31, except in the first year, when the withdrawal must take place no later than April 1.

A word of caution: If you do not make the scheduled withdrawals after age $70\frac{1}{2}$, you will be penalized by 50 percent of the deficiency.

> *Example:* You are required, according to the life expectancy tables, to withdraw $7,000 from your IRA this year. You withdraw only $2,000. The IRS assesses the 50 percent penalty on the difference of $5,000. The penalty amount: $2,500.

The Exclusion Ratio

To determine what portion of the total in the IRA may be excluded from tax, you apply an exclusion ratio to each year's withdrawals. This is a similar procedure to the one used for tax-deferred annuities. The calculation is summarized in the worksheet in Figure 6-1a. Note that this shows

---

A: Total of nondeductible contributions, less any
    tax—free withdrawals previously taken $_____

B: Total value of IRA at end of year $_____

C: Total distributions taken during the year $_____

D: Step B + Step C $_____

E: Step A + Step D   _____

F: Step C x Step E = non—taxable distribution $_____

G: Step C − Step F = taxable distribution $_____

FIGURE 6-1a Worksheet: Taxation of IRA Withdrawals

both the amount that is not taxed and the amount that is taxed for the year.

> *Example:* Your IRA is currently worth $85,000, and you withdrew $6,000 during the past year. The total of contributions made over the past 25 years was $50,000, none of which was claimed as a deduction against adjusted gross income.

In this example, the contributions were not tax-deferred, since no current-year tax benefit was ever claimed. However, accumulated earnings have increased the value of the account. A filled-in example of the worksheet is shown in Figure 6-1b.

In the following year, the first value would be reduced by the amount of nontaxable distributions, or $3,297. Thus, instead of using $50,000, the "A" total would be $46,703. The account's year-end value would grow as the result of any earnings accumulated during the year, and it would be reduced by the amount of subsequent withdrawals. The calculation would continue until all nondeductible contributions were used up. From that point on, all withdrawals would be fully taxed.

If the entire value of contributions had been used to reduce each year's adjusted gross income, then all withdrawals would be taxed. This brings up the planning point mentioned earlier. In any year that you do not need the deduction (such as years in which your taxable income is relatively low), it could be advantageous to make contributions but not take a deduction. Then, when withdrawals do begin years later, you will have a larger exclusion base.

A Total of nondeductible contributions, less any tax-free withdrawals previously taken	$ 50,000
B Total value of IRA at end of year	$ 85,000
C Total distributions taken during the year	$ 6,000
D Step B + Step C	$ 91,000
E Step A + Step D	.5495
F Step C x Step E = non-taxable distribution	$ 3,297
G Step C - Step F = taxable distribution	$ 2,703

FIGURE 6-1b Worksheet: Taxation of IRA Withdrawals

Where to Open the IRA

The most popular institutions for opening IRA accounts are banks or savings and loan associations, mutual fund companies, and brokerage firms.

The advantage of savings institution IRA accounts is simplicity. Interest-bearing accounts can be opened as part of your IRA in time deposit certificates, money market accounts, or passbook savings accounts. The disadvantage is lack of diversification and growth. Your money may earn and compound interest, but there is no opportunity for achieving capital gains in such accounts.

Mutual funds are diversified by nature. The fund's management invests a pool of capital professionally, buying in a wide range of stocks or bonds, or both. You may have the privilege of switching IRA money from one fund to another within a family of funds. And long-term income and growth will be rewarding, assuming that future patterns follow historical ones.

Brokerage accounts are for the most sophisticated and for those willing to assume greater risks. Investing in common stocks, bonds, and other exchange market products may provide the greatest opportunity for growth, as well as the greatest exposure to loss.

Many IRA accounts are opened through brokerage firms and are self-directed: The brokerage firm acts as custodian, but you decide where and how to invest your money. Portions can be placed in common stocks, bonds, mutual funds, market market funds, covered options, real estate investment trusts, and a range of other products offered by the firm and approved for IRA investors.

Before opening any IRA acccount, you should compare annual fees. Banks and mutual funds charge minimal fees per year, and a self-directed account should average between $25 and $50 per year. Avoid any arrangement in which there is a minimum fee plus a fee based on the account's value. Also avoid situations in which you are charged transaction fees beyond the normal brokerage commission each time you buy or sell. Some trust companies are very expensive, and paying excessive fees is not necessary. You can open self-directed accounts with most national brokerage firms without paying extra fees.

The advantage of the self-directed account is that you can invest a growing amount of capital in a number of different ways without having to open new accounts to achieve the same result. Some people have diversified by opening different IRA accounts each year. This choice becomes complicated and unnecessary, for several reasons:

1. *Management becomes difficult.* Having to watch a number of different IRA accounts each year will become a management burden when you have ten or more different accounts. It is much simpler to have all IRA money in one place.
2. *Annual fees will be excessive.* Even if fees are only $5 per year in each account, you will be paying far too much when you open a different account each year.
3. *Withdrawal accounting will be complicated.* It is complicated enough accounting for taxable and nontaxable portions of one IRA each year. With a number of accounts, you will lose flexibility and add to the complexity of the annual calculation and reporting chore.
4. *The same result is possible in one account.* You can diversify your money without a number of different accounts through a self-directed IRA. The fee may be higher than the fee for each individual account, but it will become less significant as the value of the IRA grows each year.

Transfers and Rollovers

If you currently have multiple IRAs or if you want to change custodians or trustees, you are allowed to transfer funds whenever you want. A *transfer* should not be confused with a *rollover*, which is much different.

There are two ways to transfer IRA funds. First, you may close one account and then reinvest the full amount. If you take possession of the money, you must reinvest it within 60 days or you will lose the tax deferral and be subject to the 10 percent early withdrawal penalty. The second method is to open an account with a new trustee and then direct the old trustee to transfer funds. With this method, you never take possession of the funds.

A rollover occurs when you transfer money from another qualified plan into a special *rollover IRA*. If you are funding an IRA each year and you effect a rollover, you should keep the two funds separate.

Example: After working for one employer for a number of years, you leave your position. When you leave, you receive a lump-sum distribution representing your vested value in the company retirement plan. You establish a rollover IRA within 60 days and deposit the full amount into it. By taking these steps, you continue to defer taxes.

There is no dollar limit to a rollover IRA, as there is with the normal variety. Another feature of the rollover account is that it can be rolled again, into another qualified plan.

Example: A few months after establishing your rollover IRA, you take another position. You are allowed to move the funds in the rollover IRA into the new employer's retirement plan without any tax consequences.

If you mingle rollover and nonrollover IRA funds, you lose the privilege of moving the money a second time. Moreover, once the mingling occurs, the total fund must be left intact or tax deferral privileges will be lost.

It might not always be in your best interests to continue tax deferral when you receive a lump-sum distribution. You may qualify for averaging of the tax, which reduces the liability. This privilege is not given to IRA accounts.

Example: In the year you receive a lump-sum distribution, you have very little earned income. As an alternative to setting up a rollover IRA, you decide to pay the taxes now and to use the special five-year averaging provision to minimize the tax.

Disadvantages of the IRA

As attractive as tax deferral is to many people, IRAs come with distinct disadvantages:

1. *Loss of current deduction.* For many, IRAs have lost their appeal. Since full deductibility was allowed in the past, today's rules make the IRA much less attractive.
2. *The 10 percent penalty.* The tax and penalty consequences of early withdrawal make IRA funds generally unavailable—or available only at very high cost. Any money placed in an IRA account should be earmarked for later years. If you think you will need to withdraw funds before age $59\frac{1}{2}$, do not open an IRA.
3. *Retirement is a remote occurrence.* A number of people view retirement as a very distant event and not something to plan for today. The earlier you begin planning, the more secure your retirement years will be. However, this advice is more easily given than taken.

4. *Penalty for overcontributions.* If you contribute more than you are allowed in any one year, you are subject to a 6 percent tax penalty on the amount. The overcontribution can be withdrawn or held over and applied to the next year.

5. *The 50 percent penalty.* Once you reach age $70\frac{1}{2}$, you *must* take out no less than the scheduled amount each year. If you do not, the difference is subject to a 50 percent tax penalty.

6. *Tax deferral is lost for prohibited transactions.* IRA investing is restricted in a number of ways. You will lose the tax deferral privilege and be subject to the 10 percent penalty if you engage in the following prohibited transactions:

   a. Borrowing money from your IRA.
   b. Pledging the IRA as collateral on a loan.
   c. Selling property to the IRA account.
   d. Receiving payment for managing your own IRA.
   e. Investing in collectibles or other unallowed products. (You are allowed to invest in gold and silver coins issued by the U.S. government.)

ACTION CHECKLIST

Your IRA

1. Find out the current rules of IRA deductibility for your tax status.
2. Put $2,000 per year into an IRA for deferral benefits, even if you cannot deduct the contribution from gross income.
3. Compare taxable with tax-deferred yield. Then consider IRA investing with the liquidity risk and tax consequences in mind.
4. Coordinate your IRA with other elements of your portfolio. Remember, tax status is only one aspect of the whole picture.
5. Look into alternative accounts well before the deadline to open your IRA. Consider a flexible, self-directed plan for low costs and maximum flexibility.
6. Learn the rules for transfers and rollovers. Be sure you comply before moving money out of your IRA.
7. Be aware of the disadvantages and limitations of the IRA before you place money in one.

Other Qualified Plans

Besides the individual retirement account, a number of other qualified plans are available:

1. *Keogh plan*. The Keogh plan is available to self-employed individuals. As much as 20 percent of net income from self-employment can be contributed each year, up to a maximum of $30,000 per year.
2. *Simplified Employee Pension*. The SEP is available to self-employed individuals or corporate employees. A SEP-IRA can be entered into by employees age 21 or older who have worked for an employer at least three of the last five years. Employers invest money as the employee directs. The maximum contribution is 13.04 percent of income, up to a maximum of $30,000 per year.
3. *401K plan*. This is an employee profit-sharing plan with a salary reduction feature. Employers may add additional money based on the amount the employee has deducted each pay period. The tax-deductible amount is adjusted each year according to the cost of living index.
4. *403B plan*. This is generally available to employees in education and nonprofit organizations. Employers often add funds based on the amount employees have taken from their paychecks. Proceeds are used to purchase tax-deferred annuities. The annual maximum is adjusted for cost-of-living increases.

The individual retirement account and similar qualified plans offer long-term tax deferral, often with great flexibility. However, even without the IRA, you can achieve deferral. The next section explains methods of gaining tax deferral through savings bonds, other zero coupon bonds, and additional products you can use to structure your personal financial plan.

SECTION THREE

Tax Savings, the Traditional Approach

CHAPTER 7

From EE to HH

Some investments have undeservedly poor reputations, often because they are relatively unexciting. One example is the *United States savings bond*. It is very safe, it requires no real maintenance, and it guarantees a minimum rate of interest.

A widespread perception is that savings bonds yield too little to be considered seriously. Financial advisers may not recommend this investment because they will earn no commission. And since there is so little risk involved, many investors do not give government bonds a second glance. However, savings bonds offer a combination of attractive features that could make them appropriate for your portfolio.

Be aware of the danger involved in attraction to risk. You may want to include investments in your portfolio that require research and a degree of danger for a number of reasons—perhaps for diversification, higher-than-average yields, and liquidity. However, as part of the program, also review the benefits of U.S. savings bonds. These include tax deferral and, in some cases, a complete exemption from federal and state taxes; a high degree of safety; compound interest; and a choice of year in which taxes will be paid.

A major disadvantage of savings bonds is that they are nonmarketable. That means that ownership cannot be transferred from one person to another. The only way to change ownership is by cashing in the bond. For some, this feature will not pose a problem. However, for others, it is a prohibiting factor. Because savings bonds are nonmarketable, for example, they cannot be pledged as collateral on a loan. If your entire portfolio consisted of savings bonds and you needed to secure a loan, you would be required to sell part of your holdings, place the funds in a marketable security, and then make the pledge.

Series EE and HH Bonds

EE bonds are purchased from the U.S. Treasury, either directly or through a savings institution. The easiest way to buy a bond is through a bank or savings and loan association. The purchase price is one-half of the face value, or maturity value, of the bond. For example, a $50 bond costs $25. You pay this amount to the bank, and you receive a certificate on which your name, address, and social security number have been typed.

This bond certificate is not negotiable. So if it is stolen or lost, you do not need to worry about someone else cashing it in. The Treasury will replace lost certificates without charge. Many people purchase bonds each month through payroll deduction or when making a bank deposit. While in the institution, they place the certificate in their safety-deposit box.

It takes approximately $9\frac{1}{2}$ years for a savings bond to reach maturity value, and it will take less time if the interest rate is increased beyond the annual guaranteed rate of $7\frac{1}{2}$ percent. However, you are allowed to hold your bonds for a shorter or longer period.

1. You can cash in a Series EE bond at any time after a six-month holding period. The bond will earn a compounded annual rate for the entire time it is owned. You can also cash in the bond within the first six months in case of financial emergencies.
2. You can continue to hold the bonds beyond the point of maturity. In that case, you continue to earn the compound rate of interest. You also continue to defer federal tax on all interest earned.

You are only taxed on Series EE bond interest when you sell your bond. Interest is always exempt from any state income taxes.

Example: An investor owns several Series EE bonds that have matured. However, he does not cash them in until a year in which other income is relatively low. Because he is in a lower tax bracket during that year, the tax consequence is minimized. In addition, there is no state income tax due on the bond interest.

Interest is calculated and reported by the Treasury every six months. For this reason, maturity may occur before the $9\frac{1}{2}$ year mark. The higher the rate, the shorter the time required for maturity of the bond. The rate you will earn on a Series EE bond held for five years or more will be equal to 85 percent of the average yield paid on other U.S. government securities.

Comparing Bonds

As already explained, savings bonds are bought at half their face value, and the interest you earn is not paid each six months but accrues during the time you own the bond. The investment gains value every six months, when interest is credited to your bond. In contrast, the more traditional corporate bond is bought at or near face value, and accrued interest is paid out at regular intervals.

> *Example:* A corporate bond investor pays $1,000 for a bond. This is face value, since $1,000 will be repaid at maturity. The annual rate is 8 percent. Every six months, the issuer pays one-half of the interest rate, or $40. When he bond matures, the issuer repays the $1,000.

In this example, the investor has a number of disadvantages:

1. *Interest is not compounded.* When interest is paid out every six months, there is no compounding. Over a number of years, therefore, the total yield from a corporate bond will be much less than that from a savings bond yielding the same or even a percentage point less. To overcome this problem, the corporate bond investor must be able to reinvest interest payments at the same rate as that paid through the bond. If market rates fall below the level the bond is yielding, the investor will not be able to earn the same rate in the future.
2. *Interest is taxed each year.* Taxation (including the possibility of both federal *and* state tax) will reduce the true rate of interest earned on the corporate bond. A savings bond, in comparison, allows you to defer the tax consequences until the bond is cashed in. This gives savings bond investors the advantage of timing: They do not have to cash in their bonds during any specific year.
3. *The investor is exposed to market risk.* A corporate bond may rise or fall in value, depending on changing interest rates. If the bond

becomes deeply discounted (if its current value falls well below face value), it can only be sold at a loss. This risk does not exist with savings bonds; the current value is always equal to the discounted purchase price plus interest accrued to date.

Of course, savings bond investors are exposed to the same interest rate risk that all bondholders suffer. If current market rates are higher than the rate you are earning on a bond (the minimum guaranteed rate is $7\frac{1}{2}$ percent), you are missing opportunities to maximize annual return. However, a savings bond can be sold at any time after six months, without penalty.

By the end of the holding period, the savings bond will reach or surpass face value. Since each individual is allowed to buy up to $30,000 per year in face value, the maximum purchase amount is $15,000. However, a husband and wife may each purchase up to that limit. Series EE bonds are available in several denominations:

PURCHASE PRICE	MATURITY VALUE
$ 25.00	$ 50.00
37.50	75.00
50.00	100.00
100.00	200.00
250.00	500.00
500.00	1,000.00
2,500.00	5,000.00
5,000.00	10,000.00

Taxes can be deferred by holding Series EE bonds beyond the maturity date. Another method is to exchange EE bonds for what are called Series *HH bonds*, which can only be purchased in this way. In that event, the Series EE interest is deferred until the HH bonds are sold. However, interest earned on the Series HH bond is taxed each year. The EE bond must have a current market value of $500 or more, and the HH bond matures in ten years.

Whereas EE bond interest is accrued, the HH bond works like the traditional corporate issue. Interest is paid every six months, without compounding, and is taxed at the federal level each year. However, there is no state tax on HH bond interest.

Example: You purchased a Series EE bond nearly ten years ago for $250. Today, the bond is worth $500. You exchange it for a Series HH bond. The interest of $250 is deferred until you sell the HH bond; however, the interest you receive twice a year on the HH bond is declared on your income tax return.

In this example, the Series EE bond interest is deferred twice: first, during the period between purchase and maturity, and second, when EE bonds are exchanged for HH bonds.

Calculating the Value

The appeal of savings bonds for many is that they are relatively inexpensive. For $25 a month (withheld from your paycheck, for example), you can create an income stream in the future of $50 a month or more. As a low-maintenance, safe investment, savings bonds are part of many portfolios.

The process by which a $25 investment is transformed into a $50 value is mysterious to many people. The point to remember is this: The higher the compound interest rate, the shorter the time required to double your money.

The $25 purchase price is called the *present value* of the bond worth $50 (see Chapter 3). Using the minimum compound rate that is guaranteed in a Series EE bond, you can use the formula shown in Figure 7-1 to establish that it takes about $9\frac{1}{2}$ years for your money to double. The full term of $9\frac{1}{2}$ years contains 19 semiannual periods. The compound rate changes every six months; so in order to compound correctly, you need to use a factor of 19 for the number of periods and to divide the minimum annual interest in half. And because a half-year earns only one-half of the annual rate, the guaranteed rate of $7\frac{1}{2}$ percent

$$PV = \frac{M}{(1 + r)^n}$$

PV = present value

M = maturity value

r = interest rate

n = number of periods

FIGURE 7-1 Formula: Present Value of a Bond

represents 3.75 percent per year. In decimal form, this is 0.375 in the formula:

$$PV = \frac{\$50}{(1 + .0375)^{19}}$$

$$= \frac{\$50}{2.01268}$$

$$= \quad \$24.84$$

Using the $9\frac{1}{2}$ years and a maturity value of $50, this exercise establishes that the present value of the matured bond is $24.84, slightly less than $25.00. Therefore, the actual maturity period at the minimum guaranteed rate is slightly more than $9\frac{1}{2}$ years. This formula will be discussed again in the next chapter, where zero coupon bonds are explained.

In practice, the half-year rates will change during your holding period for the Series EE bond. In some years, you may earn a higher rate; in others, the minimum guaranteed rate will be paid. Remember, you are allowed to cash in your bond without penalty at any time after a six-month holding period. You may also continue holding your bond beyond the maturity date or continue deferral of interest by exchanging the EE for an HH bond.

Figure 7-2a is a worksheet you can use to keep track of a savings bond's current value. This worksheet can be used for a single bond. To keep track of a series of EE bonds, you can add together previously accrued values of bonds held six months or more, or you can maintain a separate worksheet for each one.

Figure 7-2b is an example of a Series EE bond that matures in nine years, or 18 half-year periods. The faster maturity results from accrual of interest above the minimum guaranteed rate in some six-month periods.

The actual interest earned during each six-month period might not seem like much. However, remember that this is an example using a single, $50 savings bond purchased for $25. The actual earnings will be much greater if higher-denomination bonds are purchased. And if you buy bonds regularly as part of a savings plan, the overall effect is more significant.

This illustration was based on the assumption that a bond was purchased on the first day of a six-month period. In practice, you may buy a bond on any day. To calculate the first period's interest, you will

Purchase Date _____

Bond Serial Number _____

6–MONTH PERIOD	ANNUAL RATE	INTEREST	BALANCE
purchase price			$ _____
_____ to _____	_____	_____ %	_____
_____ to _____	_____	_____	_____
_____ to_____	_____	_____	_____
_____ to_____	_____	_____	_____
_____ to_____	_____	_____	_____
_____ to_____	_____	_____	_____
_____ to _____	_____	_____	_____
_____ to _____	_____	_____	_____
_____ to _____	_____	_____	_____
_____ to_____	_____	_____	_____
_____ to_____	_____	_____	_____
_____ to_____	_____	_____	_____
_____ to_____	_____	_____	_____
_____ to _____	_____	_____	_____
_____ to _____	_____	_____	_____
_____ to _____	_____	_____	_____
_____ to_____	_____	_____	_____
_____ to _____	_____	_____	_____
_____ to_____	_____	_____	_____
_____ to _____	_____	_____	_____

FIGURE 7-2a Worksheet: Savings Bond Value

need to prorate the days in the six months and reduce the total period's interest.

Example: The current rate for Series EE bonds issued between May 1 and October 31 is 8.06 percent. You purchased a $50 bond on July 16 and paid $25.

The prorated interest is based on a 360-day year and so assumes that every month contains 30 days. Thus, a six-month period contains 180 days. The period from May 1 to July 15 is 75 days (30 days each for May

Purchase Date _____

Bond Serial Number _____

6–MONTH PERIOD	ANNUAL RATE	INTEREST	BALANCE
purchase price			$25.00
____ to ____	7.5%	.94 %	25.94
____ to ____	7.5	.95	26.89
____ to ____	8.1	1.09	27.98
____ to ____	7.9	1.11	29.09
____ to ____	8.2	1.19	30.28
____ to ____	7.6	1.15	31.43
____ to ____	8.1	1.27	32.70
____ to ____	8.0	1.31	34.01
____ to ____	8.0	1.31	34.1
____ to ____	8.2	1.39	35.40
____ to ____	8.4	1.49	36.89
____ to ____	7.9	1.46	38.35
____ to ____	7.5	1.44	39.79
____ to ____	7.6	1.51	41.30
____ to ____	7.9	1.63	42.93
____ to ____	7.8	1.67	44.60
____ to ____	8.0	1.78	46.38
____ to ____	7.8	1.81	48.19
____ to ____	7.6	1.83	50.02

FIGURE 7-2b Worksheet: Savings Bond Value

and June, and 15 days for July). Thus, your first period's interest should include only 105 days (180 less 75).

Step A: Calculate 8.06 percent interest for six months.

$$\$25 \times .0403 = \$1.01$$

Step B: Reduce interest to 105 out of 180 days.

$$\frac{105}{180} \times \$1.01 = \$.59$$

ACTION CHECKLIST
_____

Savings Bonds

1. Become familiar with the way savings bonds work.
2. Start a regular investment plan to build part of your portfolio in savings bonds.
3. Compare savings bond features with features of other debt securities to make an informed decision before you buy.
4. Learn how to calculate compound rates of return on savings bonds. Apply the formula to track and place value on your own portfolio.

_____

In this example, the partial first period's interest will be 59 cents. Beginning with the second six-month period, interest will be calculated for the full term.

Savings Bonds in Your Portfolio

In determining whether or not to include savings bonds in your portfolio, keep these major features in mind:

1. *Risk is very low.* Savings bonds, like other U.S. government securities, are guaranteed by the full faith and credit of the United States. No other guarantee is considered as worthy as this. Thus, when comparing savings bonds with any other investments, you should include in your evaluation both the annual yield and the market risk.
2. *The minimum rate is guaranteed.* Savings bonds will not earn less than the $7\frac{1}{2}$ rate for a holding period of five years or more. If you cash in your bond before the five years have expired, the compound rate could be lower than this level. The actual rate earned will be higher when interest paid on other Treasury securities is also higher.
3. *Interest is compounded semiannually.* Unlike the corporate bond, which pays simple interest twice per year, savings bonds offer compound interest. This feature increases their overall yield.
4. *Federal taxes are deferred.* You are not liable for federal income tax on savings bond interest until you sell. Deferral is an important

feature, since it increases the after-tax yield from one year to the next.

5. *Deferral can be extended.* Even when your Series EE bonds mature, you can extend the deferral of income taxes by exchanging them for Series HH bonds. However, interest on the HH bond is taxed each year and is not compounded.

6. *Savings bonds are exempt from state taxes.* Interest on both EE and HH bonds is totally exempt from all state income taxes. If you live in a state with an income tax, this feature increases your after-tax yield, and other, taxable investments do not have it.

7. *Savings bonds may be exempt from all taxes.* If you cash in savings bonds acquired after December 31, 1989 and use the proceeds to fund a higher education, all interest may be exempt from tax, even at the federal level. (This benefit is phased out as income rises.) The benefit makes savings bonds ideal for planning a child's college education. Not only is the investment safe, but all earnings may be free from income tax when the bonds are sold.

The major drawback of savings bonds—the inability to pledge them as collateral—is a minor problem, of concern only to those who will need to use their investments as security. Because savings bonds can be cashed in at any time after a six-month holding period, they can be exchanged for other investments at any time.

The Treasury provides free information concerning the current yield on savings bonds. Call 1-800-USBONDS to get a quote on the current rate.

Since they are bought at half their face value, savings bonds are a form of *discounted bond.* The next chapter explains how other discounted bonds can be purchased. Zero coupon bonds, like savings bonds, pay compound interest but, in most circumstances, do not allow you to defer tax liabilities.

CHAPTER 8

Zero Coupon Bonds

The savings bonds discussed in the last chapter are one form of *original issue discount*, or *zero coupon bond*. All such bonds can be bought at a discount far below face value. Interest is compounded semiannually from purchase date until maturity, and the full face amount, or *par value*, is returned to you at the end of the term. Bonds of this sort are issued by a variety of government and corporate sources.

To understand zero coupon bonds, it is best to first consider the traditional term bond. As discussed in Chapter 7, a term bond is purchased at or near par value (a $1,000 bond costs $1,000), and interest is paid to you twice per year. In many cases, the term bond may have a current market value above par (it then sells at a premium) or below par (it then sells at a discount). The semiannual interest payments, however, are always based on par value. For example, a $1,000 bond yielding 10 percent per year will yield two semiannual payments of $50 each.

In the past, investors of term bonds clipped coupons attached to the bond certificate and mailed them to the issuer to claim interest payments. Today, investors generally do not have to submit coupons, but the interest rate is called the *coupon*, or *nominal*, *yield*. This is not the same as the current yield.

Example: An investor pays $1,000 for a term bond with a coupon yield of 10 percent. Every six months, the issuer sends a check for $50, representing one-half of the promised 10 percent rate. Two years after the bond is purchased, its current market value is $950. The issuer continues to pay $50 every six months. However, current yield is now 10.53 percent. (Calculate by dividing annual payments by current market value: $100/$950 = .1053.)

Term bonds may rise or fall in value depending on the demand for bonds yielding a fixed interest rate. As other market rates rise or fall, each bond's value is affected. If a 10 percent yield is higher than what other securities are now paying, the bond will become more attractive in the market and its current market value will rise. If other rates rise above the 10 percent yield, then the bond's current market value will fall.

The changing market value of term bonds may be a problem if you want to sell a bond before maturity. You cannot sell a deeply discounted bond without taking a loss; thus, investors who purchased bonds many years ago may be unable to sell today if the interest rate is low and market value reflects lack of demand. These investors not only hold discounted securities; the yield of the securities is below market average.

The same problem may occur with zero coupon bonds. A relatively low-yielding bond held for the long term could become less appealing in time. However, there is one big advantage to zero coupons: Interest is compounded during the holding period, a feature not found in term bond issues.

The Zero Coupon Alternative

With a term bond, you invest $1,000 and receive the coupon payment twice a year. With a zero coupon bond, the purchase is made at a discount, and interest is compounded every six months. This process is referred to as *accretion,* another term for the compounding that takes place during the holding period.

The par value, usually $1,000, is attained at the maturity date. The longer the holding period, the lower the original cost. For example, a 10 percent zero coupon bond maturing in five years will cost about $614 today. However, if you are willing to hold the bond for ten years, it can be purchased today for about $377.

The term *zero coupon* means that interest is not paid out every six months, as it is when you buy a term bond. Instead, the value of the bond is increased by the interest amount every six months.

Example: You purchase a zero coupon bond yielding 10 percent, with five years until maturity. You pay $613.91. You receive no

interest payments during the five-year holding period. At the end
of five years, the issuer sends you a check for $1,000.

In this situation, interest is compounded, or accreted. However, the
interest that is accreted each year is taxable (the U.S. savings bond is an
exception). For many investors, this is a major disadvantage. Even
though interest is not physically received, there is a tax liability, called a
phantom interest. If you are earning a modest income each year, you will
not be severely affected by this problem. However, if you have a large
number of zero coupon bonds and a large amount of taxable income, the
phantom interest could become considerable.

One way to avoid phantom interest is to purchase zero coupon
bonds through a qualified, tax-deferred account (an IRA or Keogh plan,
for example), which are immune from phantom interest. The deferral
feature in these accounts offsets the problem of tax liability.

The automatic compounding that occurs with zero coupon bonds is
attractive to investors who want to purchase bonds, since it overcomes a
problem every long-term investor faces: maintaining the same rate of
return over a number of years.

Example: A term bond investor receives a 10 percent yield, meaning she receives a check every six months in the amount of $50. In
order to maintain a compound rate of return, she needs to reinvest the $50 at 10 percent consistently, a goal that might not be
possible for the entire term.

Example: An investor purchases a zero coupon bond yielding 10
percent per year. The rate is guaranteed by contract and is automatically compounded during the entire holding period.

Another advantage of zero coupon bonds is that you can afford more
bonds for the same money. For example, if the current price of a zero
coupon bond is $333, you could buy three zero coupon bonds for $1,000,
whereas a term bond investor with the same money could buy only one
bond.

Compound Interest Examples

The price paid today for a zero coupon bond represents the present
value of $1,000. The amount is based on the interest rate and the time
until maturity.

Example: You purchase a zero coupon bond that yields 10 percent per year, with five years until maturity. The purchase price is $613.91, which is the present value of the $1,000 bond. Every six months, 5 percent will be added to the value of the bond. This represents one-half of the annual rate, 10 percent.

With five years until maturity, there will be ten semiannual periods. The accretion of interest takes place on the schedule shown in Table 8-1. The original purchase price of $613.91 gains 5 percent during the first six-month period, or $30.70. Thus, at the end of six months, the bond increases in value to $644.61. This process is continued through all ten semiannual periods, resulting in a value equal to the par of the bond, or $1,000.

If the maturity period were longer but the interest yield the same, the zero coupon bond could be purchased for much less. For example, if you purchased a 10 percent bond maturing in ten years rather than in five, the purchase price would be $376.89. Accretion would occur as shown in Table 8-2. Note that the final value is $1,000.01 because of rounding of fractional values.

These tables prove that the purchase price of each zero coupon bond is accurate. Suppose now that you are given the maturity period of a bond and the rate; how can you arrive at the price you should pay? The price is derived by referring to a compound interest table that gives the *present worth*, or the *present value* of one dollar. (Remember the discussion of present value in Chapter 3.) The table provides a factor. When this

TABLE 8-1 Bond Accretion, 10 Percent, Five-Year Maturity

MONTH	VALUE	INTEREST
	$ 613.91	$30.70
6	644.61	32.23
12	676.84	33.84
18	710.68	35.53
24	746.21	37.31
30	783.52	39.18
36	822.70	41.14
42	863.84	43.19
48	909.03	45.35
54	952.38	47.62
60	1,000.00	

TABLE 8-2 Bond Accretion, 10
Percent, Ten-Year Maturity

MONTH	VALUE	INTEREST
	$ 376.89	$18.84
6	395.73	19.79
12	415.52	20.78
18	436.30	21.82
24	458.12	22.91
30	481.03	24.05
36	505.08	25.25
42	530.33	26.52
48	556.85	27.84
54	584.69	29.23
60	613.92	30.70
66	644.62	32.23
72	676.85	33.84
78	710.69	35.53
84	746.22	37.31
90	783.53	39.18
96	822.71	41.14
102	863.85	43.19
108	907.04	45.35
114	952.39	47.62
120	1,000.01	

factor is multiplied by the par value of $1,000, the result is the dollar
amount that must be invested today.

The examples, just shown used a 10 percent rate compounded semiannually. Therefore you need to refer to a table calculating the factor at a
semiannual rate. Table 8-3 shows a small section of such a table. Refer to
the lines indicating five and ten years. The factors at those points, when
multiplied by the bond's par value of $1,000, give the purchase price of
the bond with those maturity periods.

YEAR	FACTOR	PAR	AMOUNT
5	.6139133 × $1,000 =		$613.91
10	.3768895 × $1,000 =		$376.89

Once you know the interest rate and the term, you can estimate today's
price quite easily by using present value tables.

TABLE 8-3 Present
Value of One Dollar,
Semiannual
Compounding

YEARS	10% NOMINAL RATE
4	.6768394
5	.6139133
6	.5568374
7	.5050680
8	.4581115
9	.4155207
10	.3768895
11	.3418499
12	.3100679

Proving the Calculation

A compounding illustration may seem mysterious unless you can visual-
ize how the process works. Compounding at an annual rate of 10 percent is equal to one-half of that rate compounded twice per year. Thus,
as was shown in Table 8-1, the purchase price on a five-year bond earns 5
percent at the end of the first six months:

$$\$613.91 \times .05 = \$30.70$$

In the first six-month period, interest will compound for nine additional
months (the difference between the full term of 60 months, and six
months). The number of compound periods is decreased for each subsequent period, as shown in Table 8-4.

The multiplier of 1.05 represents the interest per one six-month period. In the first calculation, there are nine six-month periods; thus, the
multiplier applies nine times. In the second calculation, eight six-month
periods are involved. The diminishing number of periods continues
through to the last one.

The amount of interest falls each time because fewer periods are
involved in each calculation. This is an alternative method of showing
how compounding works. Interest does not actually decrease with
time. The chart shows the decreasing effect of the time value of
money.

TABLE 8-4 Compound Interest, 10 Percent, Five-Year Maturity

MONTH	INTEREST	PERIOD	MULTIPLIER	COMPOUND VALUE
6	$30.70	9	$(1.05)^9$	$ 47.63
12	30.70	8	$(1.05)^8$	45.36
18	30.70	7	$(1.05)^7$	43.20
24	30.70	6	$(1.05)^6$	41.14
30	30.70	5	$(1.05)^5$	39.18
36	30.70	4	$(1.05)^4$	37.32
42	30.70	3	$(1.05)^3$	35.54
48	30.70	2	$(1.05)^2$	33.85
54	30.70	1	$(1.05)^1$	32.24
60	30.70	0	$(1.05)^0$	30.70
				$386.16

Total compound interest is added to the amount invested to produce the total:

Interest	$ 386.16
Principal	613.91
Total	$1,000.07

The extra seven cents is the result of rounding in the compound interest computations.

To calculate each period's interest using a hand calculator, follow these steps:

Example

Step A: Enter '1' plus the decimal form of the interest rate for the semiannual period (one-half the annual rate).   1.05

Step B: Depress the "multiply" button.   ×

Step C: Enter the purchase price of the bond. $613.91

Step D: Depress the "equals" button. The result is the present value at the end of the first period.   =

Step E: Repeat step D for each subsequent period. The results are present value for each period until

maturity. (Note: If your calculator does not have a　　　　=
repeating "equals" feature, you will have to repeat
the first two steps for the number of periods
involved.)

The present value calculation can be applied to any zero coupon
bond. You need to know only the purchase value, the annual interest
rate, and the number of years until maturity. The annual rate is divided
in half to reflect the semiannual compound rate and the calculation is
repeated for as many semiannual periods as there are in the full term.

Comparing Bonds

The advantage of compounding with zero coupon bonds (as opposed to
term bonds) makes a lot of difference in total yield, partly because, with
the discount, it is possible to buy more bonds with the same money.

Example: An investor has approximately $6,000 available and is
comparing bonds yielding 10 percent per year. The interest rate is
identical for both term and zero coupon bonds, and maturity for
both is ten years. However, the choice involves six term bonds, or
16 zero coupon bonds each costing $376.89.

By spending only $376.89 per bond, it will be possible to acquire a
greater number of bonds for the same money. Table 8-5 shows that, in
addition, the total interest earned over the ten-year period will be much
greater with zero coupon bonds.

In order for the term bond investor to match the compounded return
experienced with zero coupon bonds, he or she will have to reinvest

TABLE 8-5 Bond Comparison, 10 Percent, Ten-Year
Maturity

	TERM BOND	ZERO COUPON BOND
Number of bonds	6	16
Investment per bond	$1,000.00	$ 376.89
Amount invested	$6,000.00	$6,030.24
Interest rate	10%	10%
Term	10 years	10 years
Total interest	$6,000.00	$9,969.76

each interest payment at the same 10 percent rate. There is no guarantee that this rate will be available in the future, at least not at the same risk level. For the person investing in zero coupon bonds, however, the contractual rate remains unchanged. This is either an advantage or a risk, depending on how market rates change.

> *Example:* During the ten-year holding period, market interest rates fall well below the 10 percent rate paid on the term bond. As a consequence, the semiannual interest payments earned on the term bond must be reinvested at a lower rate.

> *Example:* During the same period, market interest rates rise above the 10 percent rate paid on the bond. Now, the term bond investor is able to reinvest interest and earn *more* than the bond is yielding. In comparison, the zero coupon bond investor—who does not receive cash payments—continues to earn only 10 percent per year.

Again, whether you invest in a term bond or zero coupons, the interest is taxed each year. Because zero coupon bond investors do not receive cash semiannually, they must pay tax on the so-called phantom interest—a disadvantage when they hold a large number of such bonds and the amount of money is significant.

In comparison, U.S. savings bonds combine the advantages of compound interest on discounted purchases with the tax-deferral feature. However, the interest rate may be lower than the rates offered on taxable zero coupon bonds offered at the same time.

To make a valid comparison between savings bonds and other zero coupon issues, you should keep four points in mind:

1. *Risk.* Savings bonds are guaranteed by the full faith and credit of the U.S. government, which is considered the most reliable guarantee available. Other zero coupon issues may be unsecured or rated as higher risks. Depending on your own risk tolerance level, a comparable or even better return might become unsuitable.
2. *Interest rate.* Savings bond rates may be far below the rates offered on other securities with similar features.
3. *Maturity.* Savings bonds mature in $9\frac{1}{2}$ years or less. However, they may be held for longer periods. Other zero coupon issues may be selected with specific maturities in mind.
4. *Value of tax deferral.* How important is it to you to defer tax liabilities? Savings bonds allow you to take advantage of this feature automatically; other zero coupons are subject to tax each year. The higher the amount, the greater the burden of phantom inter-

---

ACTION CHECKLIST

Zero Coupon Bonds

1. Figure out how to compute the current value and interest rate of zero coupon bonds.
2. Compare the value of compounding with zero coupon bonds with the noncompounded returns on term bonds with comparable risk levels.
3. Become familiar with present value tables and their use in calculating current values of zero coupon bonds.
4. Remember the four key points to consider when evaluating bonds:
   a. Risk.
   b. Interest rate.
   c. Maturity.
   d. Value of tax deferral.

---

est. If your tax bracket and status will change during the holding period, this could become a very significant point.

Types of Zero Coupon Bonds

Besides tax-deferred savings bonds, a number of other zero coupon issues are available. Most of them are not tax-deferred.

1. *Municipal zero coupon bond.* Some municipal bonds are offered in zero coupon form, and the interest may also be completely exempt from federal tax. The degree of safety depends on the credit rating of the issuer.
2. *Money market bond.* The *zero CD* is a certificate of deposit offered in zero coupon form. The issuer is usually a corporation, and safety depends on the credit rating.
3. *Government security zero coupon bond.* A number of government securities are available in zero coupon form. These include STRIPS (Separate Trading of Registered Interest and Principal of Securities), CATS (Certificate of Accrual in Treasury Securities) and TIGRs (Treasury Investment Growth Receipts). All are available with government guarantees, which makes them very safe.

4. *Unsecured zero coupon bond.* Bonds that are not secured by real estate, securities, or other assets are called *debentures*. In some instances, zero coupon bonds are offered in debenture form. The Federal National Mortgage Association ("Fannie Mae"), an organization offering pools of mortgage investments, offers such debentures (see Chapter 11). Unsecured bonds may come with a partial guarantee, but they are not as safe as a fully secured or guaranteed bond.

5. *Secured zero coupon bond.* Fannie Mae also markets collateralized mortgage obligations (CMOs), which are secured by pools of residential mortgages (discussed further in Chapter 11). They are offered in zero coupon form. Mortgage-backed zero coupon bonds are also available from the Government National Mortgage Association ("Ginnie Mae") and the Federal Home Loan Mortgage Corporation ("Freddie Mac"). Most secured zero coupon bonds offered by these organizations mature in ten years or less. These are very safe investments with government guarantees.

Whether you invest in government or corporate zero coupon bonds, the built-in compounding is one of the most attractive features. A greater number of bonds can be purchased with a fixed amount of capital because zero coupons are available at discounts.

The time until maturity should be selected with specific investing goals in mind. For example, if your child will be attending college in 15 years and you plan to save for tuition, 15-year maturities are appropriate today, and 14-year maturities will be appropriate next year. If you are targeting investments toward the creation of income during retirement, first determine your desired retirement age. Then select zero coupon bonds that will mature when you will need and want the money.

The loss of deferral is a problem, however. This could make U.S. savings bond more attractive, even with their lower rates. It all depends on how important deferral is, given your tax status and income level.

You are not limited to original issue discount bonds in your search for deferred taxes and compounded rates of return: There are other investments with which you can achieve the same result. The next chapter explains alternative methods for reaching financial goals within a well-defined range of risk while also deferring tax liabilities.

CHAPTER 9

Other Deferral Methods

The deferral feature is built into certain investments or into the structure of some accounts. For example, you may buy savings bonds to defer your tax liability, and you will not be taxed on interest until the bonds are sold. Or you may buy a qualified investment through your IRA; you will then pay taxes only when money is withdrawn, no matter how much profit you earn before that time.

However, there are also other ways to defer and plan tax liabilities; you are not limited to investments containing deferral features or to investing through your IRA. As this chapter will show, even with direct purchase of stock or mutual fund shares, you can gain some latitude in deciding when and how much tax you will pay by buying and selling at certain times.

This is not to say that you should base all your decisions on tax avoidance. *Capital gains* usually occur when you decide to sell a share in a stock or mutual fund. If your investment has increased in value and you want to take the profit now, it would be poor judgment to put off selling just to avoid taxes.

The investment decision should always rule, even if that means paying more tax this year than you originally planned. Make a clear distinction between the two roles you perform. As an investor, your decisions should be based on reaching a predetermined goal. As a taxpayer, your actions and decisions are based on events as they unfold during the year and on planning as far in advance as possible to minimize the current year's tax liability. Avoid creating a temporary tax victory at the cost of more dollars in lost profits.

Example: You invested $4,000 in common stock last year, setting a goal that you would sell if and when the market value reached $6,000. It is now November and market value is above $6,000.

As an investor, you should sell the shares and take profits of $2,000, since your goal has been reached. However, this conflicts with your motives as a taxpayer. Why take a profit so close to the end of the year? Why willingly take action now that increases your liability when you can defer the expense by waiting two months? The answer is that if you do not take the profit, there is no guarantee that the current market value will hold until January. If share value falls during the next two months, you will miss the investment opportunity.

Because of the tax motive, you could unintentionally sabotage your own investment standards. A good rule to keep in mind and apply to yourself is the following:

You are better off taking profits and having a higher tax liability than you are losing those profits altogether.

Checking the numbers—even in the highest tax bracket—proves this point. If you take the $2,000 profit and are taxed at the rate of 33 percent, the tax consequence is $660:

$$\$2,000 \times .33 = \$660$$

But losing the entire profit because you waited will cost $2,000. Of course, the profit may reappear in time, but there is no guarantee that it will. You may have to wait several months or years before the market value of your stock again rises to $6,000. So the cost of delay could be $1,340, net of taxes. By avoiding the gain, you save $660 in taxes; but you also lose the profit opportunity of $2,000:

$$\$2,000 - \$660 = \$1,340$$

Timing for tax purposes is wise when you are reviewing your income and tax status from year to year, but it may lead to poor planning when you are reacting to year-end circumstances. For example, you may decide to hold profitable stocks or mutual fund shares until you retire. This is probably wise: At that time, your overall income should be lower, so tax rates will be minimal on investment income. However, if you are going through a last-minute tax review in November or December, you could make some bad investment decisions about whether to hold or to sell.

Stock Deferral Methods

The basic strategy for deferring profits on investment in the stock market is to time the sale. Stocks are equity investments available in an action market; you can buy or sell whenever you want, but only at the current market price. You have the right to take your profits this year or to defer the gain until a future year, when your liability may not be as high. Even if the liability will be equal, deferral may still be viewed as an advantage.

Applying the basic strategy, you again run into the problem of conflicting motives. As an investor, the timing you apply for taking your profits should be dictated by your goals and standards. A long-term goal may specify the year of sale. But if you are speculating—going in and out of holdings in search of fast profits—attaining the desired amount of profit is more important than the timing. In either case, deciding to sell when your goal dictates holding is a mistake. And holding just to defer the tax liability is also contrary to your investment plan.

Of course, you may find yourself in a situation in which your tax status dictates a timely investment decision. If the tax deferral or current-year savings produce profits beyond the original investment goal, then you may apply a timing strategy to control your liability.

Offsetting Losses to Gains

The first timing strategy is to take losses in stocks this year to offset other gains. That reduces the tax consequence and might also help you escape an investment that simply is not working out.

> *Example:* This year, you took profits in stocks amounting to $8,000. These gains are fully taxable. Also in your portfolio are holdings with current paper losses of nearly $6,000. By selling these holdings now, you reduce the taxable investment income from $8,000 down to $2,000. If you are in the 33 percent bracket, that reduces your liability by $1,980.

The tax savings can be viewed as a discount against the market loss. Rather than a $6,000 loss, the net, after-tax loss is only $4,020.

Taking a loss in the current year is a smart move in several situations:

1. *You will probably sell the losers within a year without offsetting gains.* If you plan to cut your losses and get out of the losing stocks within the near future, you are better off taking the loss now, for two reasons. First, that will reduce this year's tax liability. Second, if you take the losses next year without offsetting gains, you are allowed to deduct no more than $3,000 in capital losses per year. The balance must be held over until the following year, according to the tax rules.

   Example: Your total loss is $6,000. You wait until next year to sell, but you cannot deduct more than $3,000 in net capital losses. The deduction must be spread out over the next two years. Rather than being able to defer a tax liability, you are forced to defer a tax deduction.

2. *You want to free up the money invested in the losing stocks, believing you will earn a better return elsewhere.* You may have plans for using invested funds in another way. As long as your stock holdings are depressed, you cannot free up investment dollars, so you could be losing opportunities available today.

   Example: You purchased stock several years ago and now have what is called a *loss position.* The dividend yield is very low, and the market value does not change much from one month to another. If the money could be freed up, you would invest in another company. As long as the loss produces a tax benefit, it could make sense to take it now, free up funds, and make the new investment. That improves future income—assuming your reinvestment decision is wise—and also creates a current-year deduction.

3. *You may still want the loss-position stocks, and you plan to reinvest later.* You may want to claim the loss this year, but in the long term you believe the company has growth potential. In this case, you may sell and claim the loss and then repurchase the shares in the near future.

   However, be aware of the *wash sale rule.* If you repurchase the stock within 30 days, your loss could be disallowed. That would mean having to give up the carefully planned deduction, just because your timing was poor. You have two choices. You can wait 31 days or more before repurchasing the same shares, or you can buy additional shares of the same company first and then sell the original block and claim your loss.

> *Example:* You want to sell shares of stock and claim your $6,000 loss to reduce tax liabilities this year. However, in the long term, you still want to invest in the company. Alternative 1: You sell the shares, wait 31 days, and then repurchase the same number of shares. Alternative 2: If funds are available now, you first buy an equivalent number of shares, and then sell the first block and claim your loss. Taking either of these alternatives, you avoid making a wash sale.

Offsetting Gains to Losses

The second timing strategy involves the opposite: taking gains in stock investments to offset current-year losses. You can deduct no more than a net loss of $3,000 per year. If you have taken losses this year exceeding that amount, you can sell other, profitable investments to absorb the excess.

> *Example:* At the beginning of the year, you cut your losses in several stock positions, taking total losses of $11,000. You cannot claim more than $3,000 this year. However, you also have a number of stock investments with current market value well above your basis. If you sell before the end of the year, you will be able to absorb some or all of the excess loss of $8,000.

The $3,000 limitation applies to *capital losses,* such as losses experienced in investment holdings, real estate, and other *capital asset* investments. The maximum can be applied against earned income, such as salaries and self-employment income.

The benefit in taking profits to offset losses is that the two positions are offset. The net profit or loss in capital investments is what counts. The alternative is to carry the excess loss over to a future year. You may apply the same reasoning to selling profitable stocks that you apply to selling unprofitable ones. If you believe the long-term prospects dictate holding, you may repurchase shares later. If you believe that profits should be taken when they occur, then the justification for the offset is even more compelling.

To be able to claim the full amount of loss to which you are entitled, you need to keep accurate records. Keep all buy and sell confirmations received from your broker, as well as account statements. Also keep a running record of your investments, recording the description, purchase date and amount, sale date and amount, and the profit or loss. Use a worksheet like the one shown in Figure 9-1a.

Make an entry on the worksheet each time you make an investment decision, using information from the buy or sell confirmation. A filled-in example, using rounded-dollar amounts, is shown in Figure 9-1b. In this example, the investor may have decided to take the loss in "Natl." to offset the gain taken the same year in "Able." The same stock was repurchased over 31 days later to avoid the 30-day wash sale rule.

Stocks held in an IRA or other deferred account are not subject to taxation until money is withdrawn from the account. Thus, the timing of profitable or unprofitable holdings has no immediate tax consequence. You are allowed to invest in stocks through a self-directed IRA or Keogh account.

> ***Example:*** You invest $2,000 per year in your IRA, for which you use the custodial services of a brokerage firm. This year, you claimed substantial gains by selling profitable stock investments. There is no tax consequence, however, since you did not withdraw any funds from the account. Taxes will be paid in the future, when you begin withdrawing.

Stock Record

DESCRIPTION	PURCHASES		SALES		PROFIT OR (LOSS)
	DATE	AMOUNT	DATE	AMOUNT	

FIGURE 9-1a Stock Record

Stock Record

DESCRIPTION	PURCHASES		SALES		PROFIT OR (LOSS)
	DATE	AMOUNT	DATE	AMOUNT	
Able	3-15-91	$3,516	9-17-91	$5,706	$2,190
Natl.	5-21-91	4,210	11-19-91	3,115	(1,095)
CN	9-24-91	876	12-18-91	1,118	242
Natl.	12-20-91	3,200			
B & R	1-8-92	6,107			

FIGURE 9-1b Stock Record

ACTION CHECKLIST

Deferral in Stocks

1. Be completely aware of the dangers in the tax motive.
2. Do not allow tax issues to determine when you sell, but when possible, time your sales with tax consequences and benefits in mind.
3. Take a loss to offset net capital gains in the sale year. Repurchase with the wash sale rules in mind.
4. Sell at a profit when you have offsetting capital losses in the same year.
5. Keep a running stock record showing purchase and sale amounts and dates.

Option Strategies for Deferral

Two strategies employing *options* can be used to defer taxes and, at the same time, escape investment risks involved with untimely sales. Options are intangible investments. They give you the right to buy or sell stock at a specified price for a limited amount of time. However, you should not buy or sell options unless you thoroughly understand how the market works and the possible tax consequences of the transaction.

The first strategy is to use *put options* to protect the price of your stock. A *put* is a contract to sell 100 shares of an *underlying stock*. For a premium, you can buy one put for every 100 shares you own. The put option will increase in value for each point the stock declines.

> *Example:* It is December 1. You have 400 shares of stock that have doubled in value, and the best investment decision would be to sell. However, you would also like to defer the gain until next year. You may protect profits while deferring the gain by buying four put option contracts (one for each 100 shares held). The *striking price* of the put option (the price at which shares would be sold) should be close enough to current market value so that the dollar-for-dollar change would take effect in the event of a decline in market value.

In employing this strategy, you protect your position for the cost of the options while deferring taxes. If the stock does fall in value, you can sell the puts at a profit (offsetting the lost value in the stock); or you can *exercise* them, that is, sell your stock for the striking price of the puts. This price would be above the market value after the decline.

If the stock does not decline in value, you will lose the purchase price, or premium, paid for the puts. That is the insurance cost of protection. The loss is tax-deductible as a capital loss.

The second strategy involves selling covered call options. *Calls,* which are contracts to buy 100 shares of an underlying stock, are covered when you already own 100 shares. You will receive money for selling call options, and in this way you gain a degree of downside protection.

> *Example:* You own 300 shares of stock that you would like to sell at the end of the year. However, you also want to defer the profit until next year. You can sell three calls (one for each 100 shares) for a premium of $500 each. That gives you five points of downside protection. Even if the stock's market value declines by five points, you have covered the loss with the money received for selling calls.

Covered call writing limits your profit potential. If the stock's value rises, the calls will be exercised, meaning that you will be forced to sell your stock at the striking price. That would be lower than the market value at the time of exercise.

ACTION CHECKLIST

Deferral With Options

1. Learn option investment risks and trading rules thoroughly before getting into the market.
2. Use put options as insurance on stock gains you want to defer until next year.
3. Use covered call options for downside protection when you want to defer taking a profit this year.
4. Time expiration dates with tax benefits and consequences in mind.

From a tax point of view, the strategy could backfire. For example, if the stock were to rise in value, the calls could be exercised before the end of the year. In that case, you would be taxed not only on the profit in the stock but also on the amount you received for selling the calls. Even though there would be a tax consequence, however, you would still be ahead on an after-tax basis, since you would keep your profits. Your intent was to defer taxes; instead, you earn more than you expected.

The call profit is taxed in the year the call expires, is exercised, or is closed by purchase. Thus, if you sell covered calls in November with a January expiration date, you will probably defer taxes on the profit until the following year. There are some exceptions: If the calls are exercised before December 31 or if you close the position yourself by that date, the income will be taxable this year.

Option strategies are very complex and should not be used except by the most knowledgeable investors. Check with your broker and your tax adviser before buying or selling in the options market.

Mutual Fund Deferral Methods

Far less complex than options are strategies for planning and controlling tax liabilities on mutual fund investments. *Mutual funds* are managed pools of money. Even though the question of taxable income from mutual funds can be complex, you will simplify the process by keeping complete records.

Income from taxable mutual fund investments may be earned in a number of different ways. The nature of a payment or reinvested credit will determine the effect on your current year's tax, as well as on possible deferral of tax liabilities in future years.

The records you keep should track not only the date and amount of payment but also the nature of the payment. Types of payments made by mutual funds include the following:

1. *Dividends. Dividends* paid to you or credited to your share account include dividends on stocks and interest on bond investments. The amount paid is fully taxable in the year received. If you have directed the fund to reinvest dividends in new shares, you are still liable for taxes on the amount of your dividend.

2. *Capital gain distributions.* When your mutual fund sells holding and realizes a capital gain, it is shared proportionately by each shareholder. Your amount appears on your statement as a *capital gain distribution.* The capital gain is taxable in the year it is credited to your account or paid out.

3. *Undistributed capital gains.* Although it is not common, mutual funds may treat capital gains as increases in basis rather than as distributed credits or payments. When this occurs, the fund may also prepay income taxes in your behalf. The profit is not paid to shareholders; however, your share value will be increased by the proportionate value of the gain. For example, the fund may credit a $50 undistributed gain to your account and pay income taxes of $17 in your behalf. The $50 is treated as income in the year credited. The $17 is a credit for taxes paid. And the difference, $33, is the net increase in your basis.

4. *Return of capital distribution.* In some cases, the mutual fund will make a nontaxable distribution representing a partial return of capital. This is also called a nontaxable distribution, or a nontaxable dividend.

Whether you make a single deposit to a mutual fund account or a series of deposits over time, you need to keep complete records of transactions and credits. This is especially important if you have directed the fund to reinvest dividends and capital gains. Each time income is credited to your account, two events take place:

1. The amount credited becomes taxable income in the year it is transacted.

2. Your basis is increased by the amount of the credit to your account.

If you are making a series of monthly deposits *and* having income reinvested, you will end up with a large number of basis dates and amounts. This information will become critical in the future, when you sell shares and will need to figure out how much capital gain to declare on your tax return. If you keep complete records, you can reduce your tax liability because you can select which shares to sell.

> *Example:* You have been buying mutual fund shares for many years, and you now want to sell part of your holdings. However, you also want to minimize the current-year taxes on the sale. The current value per share is about $17; however, the shares you purchased many years ago averaged $8 per share or less.

If you kept complete records, you can specify which shares you want to sell now. By selecting the most recently purchased shares (those with a higher basis), you will minimize your capital gain. Of course, this also means that future sales will result in higher gains and taxes. The benefit of selection is in control. By deciding how much to report now, you can defer taxes on the balance.

Alternative Valuation Methods

The alternative methods for selling mutual fund shares give you no flexibility. For example, if you write to your fund management and instruct it to sell a specified amount and send you a check but you do not list the dates of purchase, you will be required to report capital gains on the FIFO basis (first-in, first-out). That means that the basis of your shares will be computed on the assumption that you are selling the first shares you purchased, perhaps at a cost far below more recent market values. So it is better to choose more recent purchases.

> *Example:* You have been sending $200 per month to a mutual fund for the past five years. Share value is now $27; however, when you began the program, share value was only $10. On the FIFO basis, you have a gain of $17 per share. However, if you specify that you are selling shares purchased on the most recent dates, your tax liability will be much lower, since the share price will be close to today's market value.

There is another alternative. You are allowed to compute the average basis in mutual fund shares using a formula prescribed by the Internal Revenue Service. Under this method, the basis of all shares is equalized so that your gain will be based on the difference between the average cost per share and the current market value at the time you sell. This alternative takes away the flexibility you enjoy by selecting which shares to sell. The only advantage is that it tends to equalize profits and taxes over several distribution years. To compute your average basis, call or write to your local IRS office and request a copy of Publication 564, *Mutual Fund Distributions*.

Keep complete records of all purchases. Be sure to include not only the money you send to the fund but also the income reinvested in your behalf. Later, when you want to sell part of your holdings, you will be able to select the higher-basis portions of your account. Use the worksheet shown in Figure 9-2a.

When you do write to the fund with instructions to sell, be sure to indicate which of your holdings you want sold. To the fund, the decision does not matter. It will liquidate the number of shares you specify to free up the amount you request regardless of when they were purchased. But to you, your letter is proof of your basis. The records you keep support your contention that you are not restricted to either the FIFO basis or the average basis.

A filled-in example of the "Purchases" side of the worksheet is shown in Figure 9-2b. In this example, $2,000 was invested at the beginning of the year. On the first of each month, an additional $100 was sent in. During each month, the fund credited the account with reinvested dividends and capital gains, increasing the basis in each case. The

Mutual Fund Record					
Fund _____					
PURCHASES			SALES		
DATE	SHARES	AMOUNT	DATE	SHARES	AMOUNT

FIGURE 9-2a Mutual Fund Record

Mutual Fund Record					
Fund _____					
PURCHASES				SALES	
DATE	SHARES	AMOUNT	DATE	SHARES	AMOUNT
1-1-91	119.05	$2,000			
2-1-91	5.93	100.00			
2-18-91	1.66	28.16			
3-1-91	5.97	100.00			
3-21-91	2.03	34.11			
4-1-91	5.88	100.00			
4-17-91	1.14	19.35			

FIGURE 9-2b Mutual Fund Record

monthly statement reports the number of shares and the amount of each investment. To determine the share value, divide the amount invested by the number of shares. For example, on March 1, $100 was invested, and 5.97 shares were added to the account:

$$\frac{\$100.00}{5.97} = \$16.75$$

At the time the investment was received by the mutual fund, the net asset value per share was $16.75. Because the value of the investment portfolio varies each day, the share value also changes each time an investment is credited. If the investor decided to sell part of the account several months or years later, this record would provide the information needed to select higher-basis investments and, as a result, defer taxes.

Tax-Oriented Mutual Funds

Some mutual funds are especially designed for tax benefits. For example, some funds invest only in tax-exempt municipal bonds or money market instruments. The yield on these funds will be lower than on taxable invest-ments, since income is not tax-deferred but entirely free of tax (see Chapter 13). Before buying shares in tax-exempt funds, be sure the yield is greater than the after-tax yield would be on other investments.

Capital gains realized in a tax-exempt mutual fund are usually taxable. Only income is exempt.

> *Example:* A tax-exempt mutual fund purchased some bonds at a discount. Later, when the capital gain was realized, each investor was credited with a portion of the total gain. While income continued to be exempt from federal tax, the capital gain was taxable in the year credited.

Another variety of pooled investment is the *unit investment trust (UIT)*. This is a fixed portfolio of bonds and other fixed-income products, which means that none of the holdings are sold. The UIT may be designed strictly to invest in tax-exempt securities or may also offer a range of taxable debt securities.

The UIT portfolio remains fixed, with payments made to investors when interest is received by the bond issuers and when bonds mature and the face value is repaid to the trust. The UIT schedules a stream of payments to investors over a period of years. Although this schedule may be viewed as an advantage, it could also become a problem. Since the UIT holdings are fixed, the issuer's safety rating may be downgraded at some point in the future: There is no active management of the portfolio in most instances.

Comparing Alternatives

Whether you invest money in stocks, mutual funds, or specialized tax-exempt funds or UITs, compare the deferral privilege to that of investments in which you do not enjoy the same flexibility.

> *Example:* Some of your funds are invested in a money market fund. Each month's interest income is fully taxable and cannot be deferred. The share value is also fixed at one dollar per share, so you cannot employ timing strategies; there are no capital gains to reinvest, or to plan and time. Another part of your portfolio is in the stock market, where you can control and time capital gains from one year to the next.

Diversification is an important basic principle to observe. You may need to keep part of your investment funds in a highly liquid account, but you will also give up the benefit of control over taxes each year.

A C T I O N   C H E C K L I S T

Deferral with Mutual Funds

1. Keep a thorough record showing dates for the following:
   a. Purchase amounts.
   b. Sale amounts.
   c. Dividends earned and paid.
   d. Capital gains distributions.
   e. Undistributed capital gains.
   f. Return of capital distributions.
2. Learn the tax rules for each type of transaction. Also learn the rules for determining the taxability of mutual fund sales.
3. Consider buying tax-oriented mutual funds for deferral or tax-free earnings. But compare estimated yields between dissimilar funds on an after-tax basis.
4. Become familiar with the differences between mutual funds and unit investment trusts.

In comparing investment alternatives, be aware of the degree of control you hold over timing of taxes. You can defer all income within an IRA or Keogh account, but you cannot get your hands on funds without immediate taxation and early withdrawal penalties. With direct purchases, you can decide when to take capital gains not only on the basis of when your income goals will be met but also on the basis of the current year's gains or losses.

Deferral in stock and mutual fund investments is fairly limited, especially considering that the investment motive is more important than current-year tax savings. For longer-term investments, deferral becomes a more significant question. For example, investments in real estate provide many opportunities to defer gains, even when property is sold at a large profit. The next section explains how tax planning works in real estate.

SECTION FOUR

Tax Savings Through Real Estate

CHAPTER 10

Home, Sweet Investment

Owning your own home is one of the best ways to build net worth and to defer taxes at the same time. This has been true historically, and it is still true today, even in light of restrictive tax changes.

When the housing market is slow (when prices are not rising dramatically and it takes longer to sell properties), industry watchers and financial advisers convey a very negative message. Would-be homeowners are told to wait or advised that the days of real estate profits are over. However, real estate is still a worthwhile investment, for a number of reasons:

1. *Necessity.* Everyone needs a place to live. The value of real estate ownership is twofold. First, you provide shelter and security for yourself and for your family. Second, your investment increases in value over time. This increase is achieved through gradual repayment of the mortgage debt and through market appreciation.
2. *Protection from inflation.* Once you buy your home, part of your monthly expense is fixed. With a *fixed-rate mortgage*, your payment will not change over time. With an *adjustable-rate mortgage*, your housing costs may rise but are limited to the payment required at the cap rate in the loan agreement. The only variables are property taxes, insurance, and maintenance costs. In comparison, renters are exposed to ever-rising housing costs.
3. *Tax benefits.* Homeowners have a number of tax benefits in the

form of itemized deductions. They are allowed to deduct interest and property taxes, which together represent a large annual outlay. In addition, taxes on real estate profits are deferred when one home is sold and another bought for a higher price.

4. *Equity growth.* Most people accumulate the largest portion of their net worth through buying their own home. Even those who invest or save regularly will probably end up with real estate representing 50 percent or more of their total net worth. In one respect, equity built through repayment of a loan is a form of forced savings. An equivalent result through savings may be difficult to achieve, since funds are more available to spend.

The Rules of Deferral

Federal rules allow you to defer taxes on the gain from selling your home as long as you buy or build another home within two years from the date of sale. (The new home may be built or purchased two years before or two years after the sale date. Thus, the total replacement period runs 48 months.) In order to defer the entire gain, you must buy a home that costs at least as much as the sale price of the previous home.

If you do not replace the home within two years, the entire gain will be taxable. If you reinvest only part of the sale price, the difference will be taxable. Since all of these computations are done on an adjusted basis, both purchase and sale prices are modified for the costs of the transaction: fixing-up expenses, brokerage commissions, and improvements.

You are allowed to defer taxes only once during any two-year period. So if you sell two homes within 24 months, deferral is based on the cost of the latest home purchased.

Example: You sold your original home 20 months ago and immediately purchased another one. Your gain of $35,000 was deferred, since the replacement home cost more than the sales price of the previous home. However, you recently sold the second home, realizing a profit of $15,000, and bought a third home.

In this example, there are three homes: the original, the second one, and the most recent. The deferral rules apply between homes 1 and 3. Any profit earned on the investment in the second home is fully taxable in the year of sale.

Example: Assume the following breakdown of each home's purchase and sale price:

	HOME #1	HOME #2	HOME #3
Purchase price	80,000	85,000	120,000
Sale price	115,000	100,000	
Profit	35,000	15,000	

Because the third home was purchased within the two-year period, the profit on the second home is not deferrable. You will be taxed on the $15,000 gain. However, the $35,000 profit on the first home is fully deferred, because you reinvested the entire sales price. The third home, valued at $120,000, is higher than the first home's sale price of $115,000.

Reporting rules for the sale of a home are more complex than for most transactions because you will not always know when or if you will replace a home that was sold. You might rent, buy a new home, or have one built. Or you might make one decision at the time of sale and change your mind within the two-year deadline.

Form 2119, "Sale of Your Home," is filed with your tax return for the year of the sale, regardless of your plans to replace the home. The rules for filing are as follows:

1. If you plan to replace the home but have not done so by your filing deadline, you fill in only part of the form but do not report a taxable gain.
2. When you do replace your home within the two-year period, you file a second Form 2119, with all information now complete.
3. If your new home cost at least as much as the adjusted sale price of the old home, no tax is due. However, if the new home cost less, you will need to amend your previous tax return and pay additional tax.
4. If you intend to replace your home but do not do so by the end of the two-year period, the entire gain will be taxed.
5. If you did not intend to replace your home, you probably paid taxes on the gain. If you change your mind and buy another home within the two-year deadline, you need to file an amended return and request a refund.
6. The cost of your new home is adjusted for any capital improvements made within the two-year period. For example, suppose you purchase a home for $95,000 and then spend an additional $25,000 to add a new bedroom. The $25,000 is added to the cost as long as it is paid within the two-year period.

Because the period in question extends beyond a single tax year, the actual outcome of the transaction is often unresolved for a considerable period of time. This is especially true if you plan a number of capital improvements to a newly purchased home.

Reporting the Gain

Form 2119 is the form you attach to your return to report the details of your transaction. On this form, three separate values are computed:

1. *Taxable gain.* This is the portion of your gain that is taxable in the current year. It applies when you do not replace a home or when the new home's purchase price is lower than the old home's adjusted sale price.
2. *Deferred gain.* Part or all of your gain will be deferred if you buy a new home.
3. *Adjusted basis.* When you defer part of your gain, your basis in the new home is reduced by the amount of gain deferred. Thus, when you later sell the home, your capital gain will be increased by the deferral amount.

Example: You purchased your first home several years ago, for $42,900. During the past year, you sold the home for $135,000, and you had sale expenses totaling $9,600 and fixing-up expenses of $2,400.

You have just purchased a new home for a price of $72,000, which is lower than the sale price of your previous home. Part of your gain will be taxed, and part will be deferred.

In this example, you need to compute the three needed results: taxable gain, deferred gain, and adjusted basis (of the new home). As a first step, you can summarize the information already known from the example:

Selling price, old home	$135,000
Expenses of the sale	9,600
Basis of the old home	42,900
Fixing-up expenses	2,400
Purchase price, new home	72,000

The procedure used on IRS Form 2119 computes all of the needed results in 11 lines. The computation in that format would be as follows:

1. Selling price of home	$135,000
2. Less expenses of sale	9,600
3. Amount realized (1 less 2)	$125,400
4. Less basis of home sold	42,900
5. Gain on sale (3 less 4)	$82,500
6. Fixing-up expenses	2,400
7. Adjusted sale price (3 less 6)	$123,000
8. Cost of new home	$72,000
9. Taxable gain (7 less 8)	$51,000
10. Gain to be deferred (5 less 9)	$31,500
11. Adjusted basis, new home (8 less 10)	$40,500

Because the new home cost less than the adjusted sales price of the old home, part of the gain ($51,000) is subject to tax. The balance of the gain is deferred, and the new home's basis is reduced by the amount of the deferred gain.

The same computation may be done on a three-column worksheet that makes the process more comprehensible. Use the worksheet shown in Figure 10-1a for this purpose. In this example, the same figures are

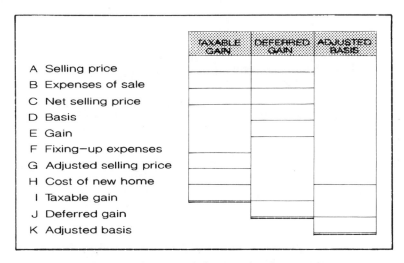

FIGURE 10-1a Worksheet: Sale of a Home

		TAXABLE GAIN	DEFERRED GAIN	ADJUSTED BASIS
A	Selling price	$135,000	$135,000	
B	Expenses of sale	−9,600	−9,600	
C	Net selling price	125,400	125,400	
D	Basis		−42,500	
E	Gain		82,500	
F	Fixing–up expenses	−2,400		
G	Adjusted selling price	123,000		
H	Cost of new home	−72,000		$72,000
I	Taxable gain	51,000	−51,000	
J	Deferred gain		31,500	−31,500
K	Adjusted basis			$40,500

FIGURE 10-1b Worksheet: Sale of a Home

broken down into three separate columns. Now you can see clearly how each result is derived. A filled-in worksheet, using the same numbers as in the example, is shown in Figure 10-1b.

The cost of the new home is $72,000; however, its basis is only $40,500, reflecting the deferred gain from the previous sale. This adjusted basis of $40,500 is carried forward and applied to the new home. When that home is sold, the lower basis causes a greater capital gain.

Example: Three years after the home was purchased for $72,000, the owner sold for $80,000 and did not replace the home. If there had been no previous gain deferral, the taxable gain would have been only $8,000. However, because the basis was lower, the owner reported a capital gain of $39,500, computed by subtracting the adjusted basis from the sale price:

Sale price	$80,000
Less adjusted basis	40,500
Taxable gain	$39,500

Another way to explain the $39,500 is to show that it is the sum of the current gain and the deferred gain:

Current gain	$ 8,000
Deferred gain	31,500
Total reportable gain	$39,500

If you purchase and sell a series of homes over your lifetime, it is entirely possible to defer gains from one home to another and never incur a tax liability. This is a major benefit of investing in residential real estate. However, the two-year restriction does apply. If any two sales are closed within 24 months of one another, the deferral is not allowed. Another restriction is that the deferral benefit applies *only* to your principal residence, which is the home you have lived in at least three out of the last five years. You may have only one principal residence, and deferral does not apply to secondary or vacation homes.

If you rent out part of your home or use part of it for a home office and claim deductions, that part of the home's value is also excluded from deferral of gain.

Example: You sold your home for $135,000 this year. However, one bedroom, representing 20 percent of total floor space, was rented out. You claimed depreciation and deducted 20 percent of maintenance, insurance, and taxes as rental expense. When you compute your gain, 20 percent will be excluded from the deferral provision.

The Over-55 Exclusion

Another tax benefit is allowed to anyone over age 55. This is a once-in-a-lifetime *over 55 exclusion* of capital gains up to $125,000. If either you or your spouse are 55 or older, you may claim this exclusion when you sell your home. The benefit is of great value to people who, upon retirement, decide to sell their home and move to an apartment, a smaller, cheaper home, or a mobile home.

Example: You and your spouse are both over age 55 this year. You have decided to sell your home and move to an apartment. The net gain on the sale is $147,000. If you elect to use your once-in-a-lifetime exclusion, $125,000 is free of tax; only the excess, $22,000, will be taxed this year.

The exclusion rule allows you to escape taxation on the equity you have built up over many years. It can be used to time a sale for maximum benefit. However, because it is allowed only once, the timing may be critical.

Example: A couple sold their home this year and purchased a smaller home. The taxable gain is $78,000. They may use their exclusion, or they may elect to pay taxes on the taxable gain because they are anticipating a greater profit in the future, when the new home will be resold.

Many people above age 55 decide to transfer their assets to their children and then remain in their homes as renters. The exclusion rule allows this without tax penalty.

Example: A couple in their late 60s have decided to sell their home to their adult children. The price is set at fair market value. They remain in the home, paying rent at fair market value. The children gain investment value and sheltered income through depreciation. The transaction is partially sheltered from taxes because the $125,000 exclusion was applied to the gain.

The Investment Side of Home Ownership

As just described, you can time and plan your real estate investments with taxes in mind. With the combination of deferral of gain and ongoing tax deductions, the tax benefits of home ownership are considerable.

However, a clear distinction should be made between the personal and investment aspects of home ownership. As a first priority, you and your family will want to own a home in a convenient, safe neighborhood. You will need access to the place you work, to schools, and to other conveniences. You and your family will become socially connected, so moving will be disruptive to everyone. If you decide to buy or sell just for investment purposes, you have overlooked the importance of personal considerations. Keeping this point in mind, you can then review the mortgage debt from an investment point of view.

A 30-year mortgage at the rate of 10 percent will increase the cost of your home by an additional 173 percent because of the high interest you pay.

Example: You purchased a home at a price of $125,000 last year, and you put 20 percent, or $25,000, down. The balance, $100,000, is financed at the rate of 10 percent with a 30-year term. The total cost of your home is computed as follows:

Down payment	$ 25,000
Principal	100,000
Interest	215,929
Total cost	$340,929

You may, of course, reduce the cost by calculating the tax benefits of interest. In the 33 percent bracket, the interest cost of $125,929 does reduce your after-tax expense to about $144,672. But that, added to the purchase price, still adds up to $269,672—much higher than the listed price of $125,000.

With the high cost of financed home buying in mind, you can begin to view your home as an investment. There are two ways to profit from investing. First is the most obvious: You can earn interest and growth on money placed in a product. Second is a less apparent method: You can reduce the cost of purchase by accelerating repayment of the mortgage loan. This technique, called *mortgage acceleration*, takes time off the loan period. Extra money is deposited (or invested) each month so that the total interest is dramatically reduced. This is allowed under the terms of all fully amortized contracts, but above 20 to 25 percent of the full loan amount, a penalty might apply.

If you are paying 10 percent on your mortgage, every dollar you invest in mortgage acceleration yields a compounded 10 percent return every year. As long as you still owe money to the lender, future interest will be reduced by the same rate. The net result is the same as if you were earning a compound 10 percent rate in a different investment.

One problem with mortgage acceleration is that it is a very illiquid investment. The only way you can get your hands on the money is by increasing your debt. That will involve a title search and a title insurance policy, an appraisal fee, and other fees the lender will charge. So once you begin a program of mortgage acceleration, you will want to be certain that you will not need to get the money back in the near future.

Two popular arguments against acceleration are flawed. First is the notion that you are better off paying your mortgage at the prescribed rate and claiming the tax deduction. When this suggestion is examined with specific figures, the flaw is obvious. You are better off making a lower interest payment over the duration of the mortgage and accepting a smaller deduction.

Example: Over the duration of a mortgage, you have the choice of acceleration. If you start the program now, you will save $85,000 in interest expenses. However, in doing so, you will also lose about

$28,000 in tax savings. After considering the tax consequences, you find that mortgage acceleration will save you $57,000.

It makes no sense to pay the full $85,000 in interest just to reduce taxes by $28,000. You are better off with the reduced interest expense.

The second flawed argument is that you can use the same money to invest elsewhere and get a better return. This point might be valid, but only if you are paying a very low fixed rate of interest and higher compound rates are possible elsewhere. Although a return greater than your mortgage rate is possible, you should also consider the risk level. Is the other investment as safe as your own home? Remember, your home is insured and will increase in value over time. In addition, you are there every day, tending the investment yourself. It is unlikely that you will be able to find an alternative investment with that degree of safety yielding a compound rate equal to the yield possible from mortgage acceleration.

The Interest Cost

Why does it cost so much to finance your home? The huge interest expense, which is well in excess of the home's listed price, is a large burden to carry for 30 years.

The reason is that interest is computed each month on the outstanding balance of your loan. So when your loan is higher—in the earlier years—most of your payment goes to interest, and only a very small amount is placed toward the principal balance. In these early years, the the loan balance declines only slightly.

Homeowners make payments according to an *amortization schedule,* which sets forth the payment period and amounts. A 10 percent loan involves .833 percent interest per month (one-twelfth of the annual rate of 10 percent). If you have a $100,000 mortgage loan at 10 percent with a 30-year amortization schedule, monthly payments will be $877.58. The first month's payment is broken down as follows:

Interest (.833 × $100,000)	=	$833.33
Principal		44.25
Total payment		$877.58

Many years later, when the principal balance is lower, the same fixed payment will be broken down differently. For example, when your remaining balance is only $50,000, the next payment of $877.58 will be divided in this way:

Interest (.833 × $50,000)	=	$416.67	
Principal		460.91	
Total payment		$877.58	

The problem, of course, is that it will take nearly 24 years to reduce your loan by one-half. Considering the size of the debt, the principal payment is an extremely small fraction of early-year payments. The last half of your 30-year loan is repaid during the last six years.

Most first-time homeowners move to a new home in about five years. But even if you stay in your home for ten years, the total of payments without acceleration will exceed the original amount of the loan.

Example: You purchased a home and financed $100,000 with a 10 percent, 30-year loan. Monthly payments are $877.58. At the end of the tenth year, you have made total payments of $105,310—more than the original amount of the loan. However, you still owe about $91,000 on the loan. Only about $14,000 has gone toward principal.

The slow rate of repayment on a 30-year mortgage is illustrated in Figure 10-2. The percentages shown at five-year intervals indicate the remaining loan balance.

One popular method of acceleration is to repay a loan over 15 years rather than 30. This is achieved in one of two ways. First, you may contract with the lender for the shorter term, which obligates you to a higher monthly payment. Second, you may contract for a 30-year term but repay the loan at the 15-year rate.

Example: You need to finance $100,000, and the lender charges 10 percent. Over a 30-year term, payments will be $877.58 per month and interest will total $215,929. Over the 15-year term, monthly payments will be $1,074.61 and interest will add up to $93,430:

TERM	MONTHLY PAYMENT	TOTAL INTEREST
15 years	$1,074.61	$ 93,430
30 years	877.58	215,929
Difference	$+197.03	$−122,499

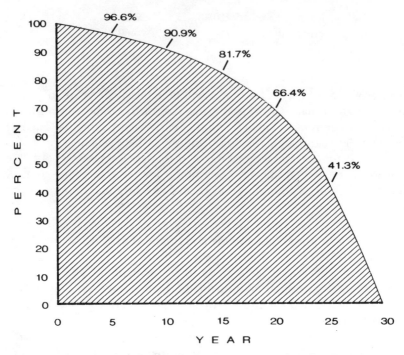

FIGURE 10-2 Remaining Balances, 10 Percent Mortgage, 30 Years

Figure 10-3 shows how dramatically the accelerated 15-year repayment affects the loan. This plan reduces interest costs substantially, but it also requires an additional cash outlay of nearly $200 a month.

Less ambitious plans are also possible. You can vary the degree of acceleration on the basis of your income from one year to the next. You could, for example, begin with a modest acceleration of $25 per month and increase the amount when you receive a raise.

Even small degrees of mortgage acceleration add up to big savings over the long term. Many years can be taken off the repayment period.

Example: You recently purchased a home for $100,000, placing $20,000 down and financing the balance of $80,000. The rate is 10 percent, and the term is 30 years. Your monthly payment will be $702.06.

Here are some facts about this situation:

1. If you make one extra payment at the very beginning of your mortgage term, the repayment period will be reduced by one full year.

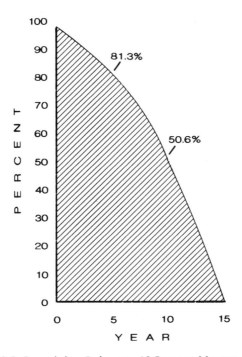

FIGURE 10-3 Remaining Balances, 10 Percent Mortgage, 15
Years

2. If you increase your monthly payment by $25 every month, you
   will take five years off the repayment term.
3. If you increase your monthly payment by $100 every month, you
   will take 12 years off the repayment term, and you will save
   $80,800 in interest.

Acceleration can be used as a planning tool. Even though you may be
committed to a three-decade repayment of mortgage debt, you can select
an earlier payoff date by increasing payments now.

Example: You plan to retire in 18 years. However, you recently
purchased a home and are committed to monthly mortgage payments for the next 30 years. Your retirement will be possible only
if you are able to eliminate this debt by your target retirement
date. With a mortgage rate of 10 percent and a balance of $80,000,
you will reach your goal by adding $100 per month to your pay-
ment. The debt will be repaid in 18 years rather than in 30.

ACTION CHECKLIST

Deferral with Your Home

1. Be keenly aware of the differences between the value of your home as your family's shelter and as an investment.
2. Learn the current tax rules concerning deferral of gain from the sale of your home. Plan sales and replacements with those rules in mind.
3. Calculate your profit and tax liability before selling your home. Remember the additional tax liability when figuring your cash flow.
4. Plan the timing of your sale with the over-55 exclusion rule in mind.
5. Calculate the long-term cost and benefit of your real estate investment net of income taxes.
6. Consider mortgage acceleration as one possible way to invest money—in equity and reduced interest costs rather than in an outside investment.
7. Review several acceleration alternatives. Seek maximum flexibility combined with the savings element.

Investing in your own home—not only through purchase but also through mortgage management—is sensible. With the combination of equity growth and reduction of interest costs, your home will probably come to represent the greatest single asset in your portfolio.

Real estate, both residential and investment, has proven historically to be one of the best investments. Although changes in tax rules concerning passive losses have severely limited the tax-sheltering benefits enjoyed in the past, some real estate investments are still profitable. If you do not have a large amount of capital, you can invest through a pool: a real estate investment trust or limited partnership. The next chapter explains how these investment products work.

CHAPTER 11

Pooling Your Money

Investors have traditionally been attracted to real estate. The historical strength and appreciation of this industry have made real estate one of the safest and most secure places to invest.

The greatest potential for profit often is found in very expensive properties, such as shopping centers, residential complexes, and industrial parks. Of course, most individual investors cannot afford to finance such multimillion-dollar purchases. In the past, real estate investment pools—notably limited partnerships—were popular for this reason. Activity in real estate limited partnerships peaked in the early 1980s, with investments often motivated by tax-sheltering benefits.

The idea of a pool is appealing. A number of investors put their money together and place it with a professional management team. This would seem to be a sure-fire way to profit from real estate. However, the history of limited partnerships and similar programs shows that there is no guarantee that you will get double-digit returns from such ventures—or that you will even recover all of your capital. The popularity of limited partnerships began to change with a series of tax reforms that started in 1981 and that culminated with the Tax Reform Act of 1986. Now, anyone interested in a real estate limited partnership as a tax shelter will soon discover that the benefits have been virtually eliminated. To enjoy tax benefits, a different method must be used. The limited partnership now has a different look. If the investment is not economically sound and if you are not willing to tie up your money for ten or 12 years or longer, than the limited partnership is not an appropriate investment.

How Limited Partnerships Work

The *limited partnership,* also called a program, is organized as a syndication. The members include one or more *general partners* (they may be individuals or firms) and a number of *limited partners,* or investors.

The general partners make the decisions. They select properties, manage them (or hire a management firm), sign leases with tenants, maintain properties, and decide when to sell. Their potential liability is unlimited. In comparison, limited partners are at risk only to the limitation of their investment.

Example: You invest $5,000 to purchase one unit in a real estate limited partnership. Two years later, a suit is filed against the partnership. The general partners may be sued personally without limitation. However, the most you could lose would be your $5,000 initial investment.

As an investor, you are a "limited" partner in a number of ways:

1. *Participation.* Limited partners cannot take part in the management decisions of the program. The general partners exercise full control. In an extreme case, the limited partners may file suit to replace incompetent general partners or to force restrictions upon them. However, as a general rule, you will have no say in running the program.
2. *Risk.* Your risks are limited, which is an important consideration. Few investors would be willing to entrust their money to strangers if, at the same time, they were exposed to unlimited liability. But although the capital risk is limited, other risks in limited partnerships are considerable. This is especially true when a large portion of the total investment is leveraged (money is borrowed), possibly placing cash flow strains on the program when vacancies are high.
3. *Taxes.* Under the rules enacted as part of the Tax Reform Act of 1986, you have very little opportunity to deduct losses from general partnerships. All income or loss from these programs is defined as *passive* (explained in more detail later), meaning that you can deduct such losses only by offsetting them against other passive gains. The tax-sheltering benefits that gave limited partner-

ships widespread popularity in the late 1970s and early 1980s have been eliminated. Now, your real estate investments must be made for purely economic reasons.

Most public real estate partnerships sell units of $5,000 or more. A private program may require investments in even higher minimums—$30,000 and up in some cases. The pooled funds of all investors are collectively invested in one or more properties, and a portion of the total goes to management fees; acquisition costs; legal, accounting, and appraisal costs; and sales commissions.

Some programs are *specified*, meaning that a particular property or group of properties has already been identified. Other programs are *blind pools*. In these arrangements, a certain type of property (shopping center, industrial park, apartment complex, for example) or a specific area of the country is identified. However, no specific properties will have been targeted at the time the partnership units are sold. If you invest in a blind pool, you cannot know whether or not a reasonable price will be paid for properties until it is too late.

Another distinction is the degree of leverage. A program may be designed to use invested capital to borrow even more and to then purchase a larger number of properties. Or a program may be defined as *all-cash*, meaning that no financing will be involved.

What to Look For

Even after tax reform, some general partners continue to offer questionable real estate programs—questionable not only in relation to taxes but also in relation to basic economics and the experience of the general partners. The following are some guidelines for selecting partnership investments:

1. *Recognize that limited partnerships are long-term and very illiquid.* Your capital will be committed for as long as ten years, often longer. The only way to close out your account is to sell your shares to one of several companies specializing in this area. And they will offer you no more than 60 to 70 percent of appraised value. For example, suppose you invested $5,000 in a partnership three years ago. Based on the appraised value of properties in the program, your unit is worth $5,500 today. If you want to sell today, you will probably be offered from $3,300 to $3,850.

2. *Find a program run by experienced, competent managers with a successful track record.* The individuals or firms acting as general partners

should have many years in the business and an established record
of successful programs that yielded profits to past investors. Also
make sure that profits in past programs were not manufactured
by selling units from an older program to a newer one at inflated
value.

3. *Seek specified programs.* Only in this way can you ensure that properties will be purchased at reasonable prices. With blind pools,
you cannot judge management's ability to pick up bargain properties in advance.

4. *Research the purchase price to ensure that it is reasonable.* Check with
lenders in the area where targeted properties are located. Ask for
the average cost per square foot for similar properties. Make sure
that the partnership does not plan to pay a price exceeding a fair
average.

5. *Check the management and sales fees involved in the program.* At least
85 percent of the money you invest should go into property purchases, with no more than 15 percent going for management fees,

ACTION CHECKLIST

Real Estate Limited Partnerships

1. Learn the rules for investing in limited partnerships.
   Be aware of the passive loss limitation.
2. Be aware of the ways you will be limited:
   a. Participation.
   b. Risk.
   c. Taxes.
3. Be aware of the illiquidity in the limited partnership
   market. There is no secondary market for your units.
4. Seek experienced management for limited partnership
   investments.
5. Make sure the investment profile of the program
   matches your own investment goals.
6. Invest only in specified programs. Avoid real estate
   blind pools.
7. Compare management fees between programs. No
   less than 85 percent of the money you invest should
   go into properties.
8. Invest in all-cash programs to minimize risks, rather
   than in highly leveraged programs.

sales charges, and other payments to general partners, sales-people, or outside consultants (lenders, attorneys, accountants).
6. *Check the schedule of profit sharing planned in the program.* When do the general partners begin to take a share of the profits? You should get back at least 95 percent of your original investment *before* the general partners begin taking a share. And then the split should be at least 80-20 in your favor.
7. *Invest in all-cash programs rather than those that plan to leverage the pooled capital.* The risks are considerably lower. If part of the purchase price is financed, you must maintain occupancy at a higher level just to afford mortgage payments; much of the increase in future market value will be offset by interest costs. In an all-cash program, running costs are limited to property taxes, insurance, maintenance, and management fees.

Master Limited Partnerships

The Tax Reform Act of 1986 created a new form of real estate investment pool called the *master limited partnership (MLP).* This is a corporation created to act much like a mutual fund specializing in real estate. Investors buy shares which can be traded publicly, just like the stock in a listed company. This feature solves the problem of illiquidity in the limited partnership. However, the market value of a share varies according to current yield, not according to asset value. This feature limits the potential for appreciation, making MLP shares act much like bonds and less like stocks.

The MLP is not taxed at the corporate level but is required to pass through profits to investors each year. All income and loss generated by an MLP are considered passive income, so losses can be deducted only to the extent that they are used to offset passive gains.

There are three types of MLP programs:

1. *Roll-in program.* A roll-in MLP buys properties with the objective of creating current income and longer-term growth. The program may offer additional shares to investors after it is created, in which case it takes on features of roll-out programs.
2. *Roll-out program.* The MLP corporation may spin off some of its real estate holdings, selling shares to investors. It creates an investment program or a series of programs and then sells partial ownership to individuals.
3. *Roll-up program.* The greatest investment risks take place in this variety of MLP. The corporation buys units in real estate syndications, combining them to create single programs or pools. The

problem is that troubled syndications may be purchased in this way. For example, you may invest in a roll-up program and later discover that the corporation purchased a number of poorly managed programs that bought properties at greatly inflated prices.

Real Estate Investment Trusts

The MLP is too closely associated with real estate partnerships for many investors. Some of these programs are no more than transfers of troubled assets from an illiquid form to a publicly traded one; in many cases, the economic problems are still there.

One alternative is the *real estate investment trust (REIT)*. These programs have historically yielded decent returns to investors, and, depending on the type of REIT in which you invest, risks can be minimal.

The REIT was created by an act of Congress in 1961 to encourage public investment in real estate. No less than 95 percent of annual income is passed to investors each year in the form of dividends. The money of a large number of investors is pooled in the trust, with each investor holding *shares of beneficial interest*. These shares are traded publicly, just like the stock of a corporation. REITs that are planned to last a specified number of years (usually ten) are called *finite-life REITs*. Those that do not specify a liquidation date are called *REITs in perpetuity*.

There are three types of REITs:

1. *Equity REIT.* This program invests directly in properties, buying the building and land itself. The value of the investment is secured by the equity position.
2. *Mortgage REIT.* This REIT uses invested capital to lend money, either for construction of properties or for existing real estate. The construction REIT was very popular in the early 1970s, but by 1974 problems began. Many developers walked away from properties, leaving mortgage REITs and their investors in trouble. Market value fell in many programs, and the publicity affected the popularity of *all* REIT programs.
3. *Hybrid REIT.* A relatively new form of REIT combines the features of equity and debt. Since most of these programs avoid construction financing and lend money only on existing properties, they are generally less risky for investors. Some hybrid programs specify the ratio of equity and debt investments that will be made during the life of the trust, which further protects investors from excessive lending risks.

One factor that prevents many people from placing capital in REITs is the relatively low commission paid to salespeople, which averages only 8 percent or less. Since other products, including mutual funds, produce higher commissions, salespeople often do not recommend REITs, even for clients seeking real estate investments and a high degree of liquidity.

The popularity of REITs has changed drastically since their introduction in 1961. During the 1960s, when the product was relatively new and the real estate market more predictable than it has been since, investors were slow to place money in the new product. In the early 1970s, REITs grew in investor popularity until the 1974 crash in the mortgage REIT market. Between 1983 and 1986, investment dollars grew substantially. With the stock market crash in 1986 and lack of financing on certain mortgage REITs, investment volume fell off again. In 1989 and 1990, the market in real estate was very slow, a condition reflected in REIT investments for the same period. Total dollars invested in real estate investment trusts from 1983 to 1989 were as follows:

YEAR	AMOUNT
1983	$750 million
1984	$2.7 billion
1985	$4.3 billion
1986	$4.7 billion
1987	$2.9 billion
1988	$3.1 billion
1989	$1.5 billion

Because real estate is a cyclical investment, the statistics do not necessarily indicate a trend. As national real estate prices rise and fall, the popularity of any real estate investment product will follow suit.

To a degree, the annual rate of return on REIT investments follows the investments trends. During the same seven-year period, the annual returns from REITs were as follows:

YEAR	RETURN
1983	24.51%
1984	13.09%
1985	5.31%
1986	18.78%
1987	−10.68%
1988	12.03%
1989	−0.51%

Mortgage-Backed Securities

Another form of pooled investment in real estate is the *mortgage-backed security,* or mortgage pool. This program acts like an income-oriented mutual fund specializing in the secured (backed by the collateral value of real estate) mortgage market. The Government National Mortgage Association (GNMA), also known as "Ginnie Mae," purchases mortgages issued by the Federal Housing Administration and the Veterans Administration, and organizes them in pools. Shares in the pools are then sold to investors.

Each investor receives a portion of interest as it is paid by the borrowers. Both the rate of return and the liquidation date are predictable, since interest payments are scheduled. The investment is secured by the residential real estate itself. In addition, investments in a Ginnie Mae fund are guaranteed by the U.S. government, considered the best guarantee available. The minimum initial investment is $25,000; you may also purchase existing shares for lower amounts, depending on the amount of income already paid out from the pool.

Another company offering mortgage pools is the Federal National Mortgage Association (FNMA), or "Fannie Mae." This company buys mortgages issued by the Federal Housing Administration, the Farmers Home Administration, and the Veterans Administration. Although Fannie Mae investors are not given the same guarantee as the one offered through Ginnie Mae, risks are not much greater.

Tax Rules

If you invest in pooled real estate programs, the tax benefits are very restricted. Tax reform occurring between 1981 and 1986 eliminated the tax-sheltering features which, before the 1980s, generated billions of dollars in limited partnerships and other programs.

In order to write off real estate losses, you must be an *active investor.* That means you must own no less than 10 percent of a property or program, and you must have the power to make decisions concerning tenants, leases, rents, and management. You may hire others to manage property for you; however, you must be directly in control of the investment.

Even active investors are limited in the amount of loss they can deduct each year. The maximum is $25,000. This maximum is available if your adjusted gross income is $100,00 or less. Above that level, the deductible total declines by one dollar for every two dollars in adjusted gross income.

Example: You have a total loss from active real estate investments this year of $32,000. If your adjusted gross income is less than $100,000, you can deduct the maximum of $25,000. The balance of $7,000 must be carried over and applied to future years.

If your adjusted gross income is between $100,000 and $150,000, the deductible limit is reduced by one dollar for every two dollars of AGI.

If your adjusted gross income is $150,000 or more, you cannot deduct losses. They must be carried over to future years.

By contrast, a *passive investment* is defined as any trade or business in which you do not materially participate. Passive activities include the investment and rental of real estate not managed and controlled on a regular, continuous, and substantial basis. Passive losses—such as in limited partnerships—are deductible *only* to the extent that you have offsetting passive gains. They cannot be applied against salaries, self-employment income, or other "earned" income in the same year. Passive losses not deductible in the current year can be carried over and applied to future passive gains.

The passive loss rule, by itself, eliminates the tax-sheltering features that once made real estate limited partnerships so popular. Because they combined high interest expenses and depreciation, investments in real estate programs used to be sheltered to such an extent that a wealthy investor could eliminate a tax liability altogether. Now that is no longer possible.

Depreciation is the gradual writing off of capital assets over a specified period of time, called the *recovery period.* In the past, real estate investments could be depreciated on an *accelerated* basis; that is, depreciation during the early years was higher than in later years. Under provisions of the Tax Reform Act of 1986, real estate investments are depreciated on a *straight-line* basis, meaning that property is depreciated evenly over a number of years. No accelerated depreciation is allowed. Residential property is depreciated over 27.5 years, and commercial property is depreciated over 31.5 years. The formula for straight-line depreciation in each case is shown in Figure 11-1.

RESIDENTIAL

COMMERCIAL

$$d = \frac{cost - land}{27.5}$$

$$d = \frac{cost - land}{31.5}$$

FIGURE 11-1 Formula: Straight-Line Depreciation

Example: You invested $135,000 in rental property last year. This is residential real estate, so the depreciation is computed on a 27.5-year basis. Land is valued at $42,000. Since land cannot be depreciated, only the balance is subject to the annual straight-line computation:

Total basis	$135,000
Less land	42,000
Depreciable basis	$ 93,000

The depreciation allowed each year is figured by dividing the depreciable basis by 27.5:

$$\frac{\$93,000}{27.5} = \$3,381.82$$

You are allowed to claim a depreciation deduction of $3,381.82 per year.

Example: You invested $200,000 in a warehouse last year. Land is valued at $48,000, and the structure was worth $152,000 at the time of purchase. Commercial property is depreciated over 31.5 years, exclusive of land:

$$\frac{\$152,000}{31.5} = \$4,825.40$$

You are allowed to deduct $4,825.40 per year for depreciation.

The depreciation allowance does provide ongoing tax shelter for real estate investors. You can shelter a portion of rental income against the annual write-off.

Example: Your rental from investing in a warehouse is $10,800 per year. However, after depreciation of $4,825.40, only $5,974.60 of the rent will be taxable. You may also deduct other expenses, such as mortgage interest, property taxes, utilities, insurance, management fees, and maintenance.

These have all been examples of *active* investments, in which you actively participate in management and own 10 percent or more of the property. The annual loss you can claim is subject to the $25,000 limit (less if your adjusted gross income exceeds $100,000).

Depreciation is always based on your purchase price plus capital improvements, and never on current market value. Even when an investment has appreciated well above your purchase level, you must base depreciation on the amount you actually invested.

Example: You purchased a house ten years ago and paid $40,000. Of this total, land was worth $10,000 and the building was worth $30,000. Since that time, you have been renting the house and collecting rent. Your depreciation is based on your purchase price of $30,000.

Five years ago, you invested an additional $15,000 to add another bedroom on the house. Your depreciation base was increased by this amount.

The house is currently valued at $155,000. Even though the market value is considerably higher than your basis, you cannot increase annual depreciation because of it. Depreciation is always computed on your basis, in this case $45,000.

You are not limited to investing in real estate through your own residence or through pooled funds: You can also purchase land or become a landlord. Additional methods for investing in real estate are described in the next chapter.

CHAPTER 12

Other Real Estate Ideas

You can find opportunities for profitable real estate investments with tax benefits in raw land, second homes, and rental property. However, you should be aware of the special risks that cannot be avoided when you become a speculator or landlord.

The following are a few sensible guidelines for investing directly in real estate:

1. *Research thoroughly.* Get the facts before buying. For local properties, check with your city or county and become familiar with the area's master plan. If a slow-growth policy is in effect, you might be prevented from developing land or converting existing property as you wish.

2. *See the property for yourself.* Never make an investment decision without first seeing the property. Real estate is not as straightforward as the stock market, and millions of dollars have been lost when individuals have purchased land in response to telephone or mail solicitations only to discover that their land was located in the middle of a lake, in a swamp, or in the middle of the desert, or that the seller did not hold legal or unencumbered title. That means that claims or liens were outstanding. Land fraud is less common today than in the past because of federal regulations; however, it does still occur.

3. *Know the rules.* Become completely familiar with the tax rules for real estate. What are you allowed to deduct, and under what circumstances? If you are not an expert in the tax law, use the services of an accountant.

4. *Select investments based on the regional economy.* Real estate values rise and fall in different ways in different parts of the country. There may be a real estate depression in one area, with no demand and falling prices, and a heavy demand and rising prices in another area. Do not base buying decisions on national trends without first checking conditions in the area where your property is located.

5. *Be aware of the risks.* The first risk is price. Remember that land prices tend to rise and fall with changing conditions by area. The local economy will dictate whether land sells at a premium or at a bargain rate.

Do not depend completely on regulation to protect you from fraud or nondisclosure. You should reasearch any investment before buying; with land, you need to become an expert in the special rules that apply.

Environmental restrictions are another form of risk. You might have specific plans for the land you buy only to later discover that you cannot achieve them. For example, local growth restrictions, hazardous waste dangers, and wetlands development bans could be in effect.

Buying Land

The strategy for speculating in raw land sounds simple: Find a lot that is very low in price in an area that is on the verge of being developed. Buy just before everyone else recognizes the emerging trend. Once development moves in your direction, the value of your land will rise, and you will be able to sell at a profit or use the appreciated value to secure financing.

This advice assumes, of course, that you are able to recognize demand and development trends well in advance of most people. In practice, selecting the most promising lots may be more difficult. Land speculation is a risky venture because the appreciation you expect might not happen for many years.

If you are looking for a future home site and are planning to eventually build on an empty lot, you may need to work with a developer. This is often necessary if you want to obtain the six basic services for the lot at an affordable price: water supply, sewage disposal, paved roads, drainage system, garbage collection, and electricity. If your empty lot is far out in an undeveloped area, it will be very expensive to provide these services on your own.

Also be aware of five guidelines for selecting lots:

1. *Shape.* The shape of an empty lot often determines its potential for appreciation. A square or rectangular lot is more desirable than an odd-shaped one.
2. *Location.* Lots in a cul-de-sac or in the middle of a block have greater potential for appreciation than corner lots or lots on busy streets. If a developer is selling empty lots in a development, avoid the primary routes into the area and select a midblock lot.
3. *Topography.* Before buying any lot, check local flood zone maps. Make sure your lot will not become a swamp the next time it rains. Also avoid lots near sharp drops, both above and below, since slides and slippage could drastically reduce the value of land. In addition, do some research to determine whether the property is located in wetlands, areas where wildlife and vegetation are protected: You could be prevented from developing such land without prior permission under terms of the Clean Water Act. You will also want to ensure that no hazardous materials have been dumped on the land you buy.
4. *Accessibility.* How expensive will it be to get water, sewage, and electricity to your property? Avoid putting your money down on a lot where you will be required to spend thousands of dollars for basic services.
5. *Price.* You can judge whether the price of a lot is reasonable by checking recent sales prices for comparable land in the same area. As a rule of thumb, the cost of the empty lot should not be greater than one-fourth of the price you will have to pay to build a home on that lot. This will vary by area, depending on demand, scarcity, and construction costs.

Buying from Developers

If you purchase a lot from a developer, ask for a copy of the *property report*. This document explains all planned and proposed improvements, which should include the six basic services. Be aware of the difference between a *planned* and a *proposed* improvement. The developer might not be contractually bound to come through on improvements that are only proposed. A planned improvement should include a completion schedule.

If you will purchase the lot under an installment contract (one in which payments are made over a number of years), title might not pass to you until the final payment has been made. In that case, get answers to the following questions: How will your investment be protected? What happens if you do not make all of the payments? And what will your status be if the developer goes out of business before you complete your payments?

If the developer operates in more than one state and sells 100 lots or more, a series of federal regulations of the Department of Housing and Urban Development protect you. In this situation, the property report must explain a number of features, including the following:

1. *Title.* The report must give the name or names of people or companies holding title, and whether or not there are any outstanding liens (whether the property is being held as security against a debt). However, even with the property report, you should still order your own title search and pay for a title insurance policy.
2. *Basic services and conditions.* The developer is required to describe planned roads, the quality of their surfaces, and who is responsible for road maintenance. In addition, the report must include the cost and accessibility of other basic services, and it must describe water quality, soil conditions, and drainage.
3. *Local services.* The availability of fire and police protection, schools, hospitals, and other services should be listed in the report. How convenient these services are may determine the future market value of the land.
4. *Association fees.* Some developments are organized with associations. Does an association exist? Is membership mandatory or voluntary? What are the fees, and who controls the association? Chances are that the developer will maintain control until a majority of lots have been sold. At that point, the owners will take over control.

Resources

Land investors need to gather information from a wide variety of sources. You cannot depend on promises made by a developer, even in print. And if you buy from a local developer or from an individual, the federal regulations do not even apply. To find out more about land investments and regulations, use these resources:

National Association of Home Builders
Phone 800-368-5242, extension 463
    The NAHB publishes literature for real estate investors, including the following:

Land Buying Checklist   — $20
Financing Land Acquisition and Development   — $32
Catalog of publications   —   free

Interstate Land Sales Registration Division
Department of Housing and Urban Development
Phone 202-708-2716
   This division regulates developers operating across state lines.
   Check for past complaints or violations. Also check with your
   state's land agency and attorney general's office.

U.S. Fish and Wildlife Service
Phone 800-872-6277 (703-860-6045 in Virginia)
   Ask for a national wetlands inventory map, which costs $1.75,
   or for a U.S. Geological Survey quadrangle map showing wetlands in detail; these cost $2.50 each. Also check with the local
   planning authority to locate local floodplains.

Environmental Protection Agency
Phone 800-424-9346 (202-382-3000 in Washington, DC)
   The EPA will supply a list of contaminated sites. Also check
   with your state's department of natural resources or environmental agency.

ACTION CHECKLIST

Buying Land

1. Remember the four guidelines for selecting empty
   lots:
   a. Shape.
   b. Location.
   c. Topography.
   d. Accessibility.
   e. Price.
2. When buying from a developer, get a copy of the
   property report. Read it completely before you buy.
3. Get literature and information from available resources, including the following:
   a. National Association of Home Builders.
   b. Interstate Land Sales Registration Division.
   c. U.S. Fish and Wildlife Service.
   d. Environmental Protection Agency.

Rules for Second Homes

Investing in raw land is far too complicated for many, especially those who want to buy a second home. In that case, you will probably seek an existing property, rent it out for part of the year and use it for vacations, or hold the property solely as an investment.

The tax rules for deducting expenses for a second home are based on the number of days rented and the portion of time the home qualifies for *personal use*. There are four instances of personal use:

1. The property is occupied by the owner.
2. The property is occupied by a family member of the owner, and rent is not being paid.
3. The property is occupied by someone other than the owner in exchange for the owner's use of another property.
4. The property is occupied by someone who is paying less than fair market rent.

Not included as personal use are days spent in repairing or maintaining the property.

The deductibility of rental expenses is based on the number of rental days. There are three classifications that determine your tax status:

1. The property is rented out for fewer than 15 days per year, and personal is less than 14 days a year. In this case, you are not required to report rental income, and you cannot deduct rental expenses. You may include mortgage interest and property taxes as itemized deductions.

   Example: You own a second home that you use during the summer and occasionally for weekends. You rent the property for one week a year. Income from the rental is not reportable; however, you are also not allowed to deduct rental operating expenses.

2. The property is rented out for 15 days or more, *and* personal use is more than 14 days or 10 percent of the rental days. In this situation, rental income must be reported, and rental expenses can be deducted to the extent of income.

   Example: You rent out your second home for several months of the year. This year, the property was occupied and rent was paid for 290 days. You spent a total of 37 days for personal use during the summer. Rental income is reported, and expenses applying to that period are deductible.

3. The property is rented out for 15 days or more, but personal use is lower than the 14 days/10 percent limitation. Rental expenses above income are deductible, but you will still be subject to passive loss rules.

Example: You rented out your second home for 212 days last year, and you occupied it for only 8 days. You are allowed to claim a loss if expenses were greater than income (for the period the property was rented); however, if it is a passive loss, you cannot deduct losses unless they can be used as offsets to other passive gains in the same year.

Landlording

When you invest in property that is rented out for only part of the year, operating expenses must be prorated between investment use and personal use. This is usually done on the basis of the number of days.

Example: Your second home was rented out for 219 days last year. You are allowed to deduct operating expenses that applied specifically to that period. For expenses that cannot be allocated specifically (such as homeowner's insurance), the deductible portion is based on the number of days:

$$\frac{219}{365} = 60\%$$

You can deduct 60 percent of your annual insurance premium as rental expense. The balance cannot be deducted.

When a single property is used partially for rent and partially for personal use, the proration is usually done on a square footage basis.

Example: You live in one-half of a duplex and rent out the other. Of a total of 3,150 square feet, you unit measures 1,701 square feet, and the rental unit measures 1,449 square feet. The rental portion of the property is calculated as follows:

$$\frac{1,449}{3,150} = 46\%$$

You are allowed to deduct 46 percent of total operating expenses against the rental income and to claim depreciation on 46 percent of the building's total value. The balance of property taxes and mortgage interest is fully deductible as personal itemized deductions, and expenses directly connected to the rental (such as advertising) are fully deductible. However, the remaining 54 percent of homeowner's insurance, maintenance, utilities, and other operating expenses cannot be deducted.

Part of your operating expenses are deductible as rental expense, and part are subject to the rules of itemized deductions. When you are a landlord, you are allowed to deduct the expenses and costs of operating the property. Capital improvements are not deductible but must be depreciated under the same rules applied to the home. The distinction between *maintenance* and *capital improvement* is based on what the expense involves. A repair maintains the property in its current condition; an improvement adds value.

Example: The roof on your rental property needs to be replaced. This is a repair, since it maintains the property in its current condition and does not increase its market value.

Example: You pay $32,000 for a room addition. This adds permanent value to the property and so is a capital improvement.

Expenses that might be considered normal maintenance must sometimes be capitalized. For example, if you purchase a room in run-down condition, you will need to do certain repairs to put the home in good enough shape to be rented out. In this instance, the expenses will be treated as capital improvements.

Normal rental expenses that are fully deductible each year include repairs and maintenance, property taxes, mortgage interest, insurance, management fees, advertising, travel, utilities, and legal or accounting fees. A special note on mortgages: You can deduct the interest but not the principal. That is repayment of the debt you incurred when you bought the property.

Deferral and Tax Sheltering

Whether you invest in undeveloped land or rental property, you should first be aware of the benefits and restrictions of tax-deferral and tax-sheltering rules. Some of these rules have been explained in Chapter 11.

Here are some more that are directly relevant to real estate investments. Land cannot be depreciated. Thus, buying lots for speculation or future development provides only a tax-deferral benefit, assuming the land's value rises over time. You are not taxed until you sell and realize your profit. If you purchase a rental home, the portion of your total cost attributed to land cannot be depreciated.

For rental property, the annual depreciation allowance provides a degree of tax-sheltering benefit. You are allowed a deduction for straight-line depreciation.

> *Example:* Your rental income is $14,000 per year. Depreciation is approximately $4,000. Other expenses add up to $9,000. Actual cash flow (income less cash expenses) is $5,000 ($14,000 income less cash expenses of $9,000). However, since annual depreciation is $4,000, *taxable* income is only $1,000 ($5,000 less $4,000).

Because payments for mortgage principal are *not* deductible, actual cash flow in these conditions can be negative.

> *Example:* Rental income last year was $14,000, and cash expenses were $9,000. You claimed an additional $4,000 in depreciation and also paid $7,000 in principal. Cash flow is negative by $2,000:

	TAXES	CASH FLOW
Rental income	$14,000	$14,000
Less cash expenses	9,000	9,000
Less depreciation	4,000	
Taxable income	$ 1,000	
Less principal payments		7,000
Negative cash flow		$ 2,000

However, the after-tax negative cash flow will be somewhat less than this, since you gain a tax benefit by claiming depreciation. For example, if you pay taxes at the rate of 33 percent, the tax benefit of $4,000 in depreciation will be $1,320, so the annual negative cash flow will be reduced to $680.00.

When is a negative cash flow justified? You may believe that your property's equity is growing at a rate greater than the negative cash flow; in this situation, it is worth the loss of cash, if that loss is affordable. In addition, part of the cash going out—in this example, $7,000— is going toward payment of the mortgage debt, which is to your benefit and not really money spent and gone. You are building equity, not only through growing property value, but also through reduction of principal.

The equity that grows in real estate is not taxed until the property is sold. However, you can tap market value growth through refinancing (replacing one loan with another), which gives you cash to invest in improvements or to use as down-payments for additional properties— all without an immediate tax consequence.

Example: You bought a rental home ten years ago at a price of $100,000. You financed $80,000, and your loan balance today is about $65,000. However, the property is now worth $150,000. You want to borrow money to make major improvements to the home. Your lender will allow you up to 80 percent of the unmortgaged current market value:

80% of market value	$120,000
Less current mortgage	65,000
Available for borrowing	$ 55,000

With rental property, the gains you realize when you sell will be taxed in the year of sale. You are not allowed to defer profits, as you are with your own residence. However, you may take advantage of the deferral provision by converting the home to your principal residence. You can have only one principal residence at any time, and in order to qualify for the deferral rule, you must use the home as a principal residence for at least three out of the last five years. Your gain will be adjusted by the amount of depreciation you claimed.

Example: You purchased your rental home for $100,000 and recently sold it for $150,000. However, while it was being rented out, you also claimed a total of $42,000 in depreciation. Your gain is therefore increased by this amount to $92,000.

This provision recaptures the depreciation previously claimed. However, as a means of deferral, it will still benefit you. Annual depreciation shelters part of your rental income each year, even though it is ultimately taxed—either when you sell that property or when you sell a property later and pay tax on the deferred gain.

To succeed as a real estate investor, you need to research local rules and restrictions and to be aware of federal rules as well. You also need to investigate and gather facts in your own behalf and to understand how the tax rules affect you. A few of these have been mentioned here. The next section explains tax rules for investors in greater detail.

Tax Rules for Investors

CHAPTER 13

Deferred and Exempt

Most investors would prefer investments that are not taxed over those that are taxed. With a tax-deferred product (such as a Series EE bond), the tax liability is put off until a future year. With a *tax-exempt investment* (such as a municipal bond), there is no federal tax at all. And some investments are not tax-exempt but include benefits that shelter a portion of your income. This chapter discusses several of these options. However, always remember that a deferred or exempt product may also offer a lower yield than a similar, taxable investment. To make a valid comparison between the two, you need to compare after-tax yields as well as relative risks.

Limitation of Tax Shelters

Before the Tax Reform Act of 1986 was passed, it was fairly easy to protect a large amount of income from taxes. *Tax shelters* enabled investors to take advantage of the law using provisions that offset taxable income through depreciation, interest, and nonrecourse financing (loans which do not have to be repaid). When nonrecourse loans could be included in an investor's basis, it was no problem to overpay for properties. The incentive was not economic growth, but tax avoidance. For example, a real estate partnership might pay a higher-than-market value for a property because the investment incentive was tax benefits rather than economic value. Nonrecourse financing justified the overpayment. Now, however, this shelter does not exist.

> *Example:* An investor purchased units in a limited partnership. In addition to investing $10,000, he signed an additional $15,000 nonrecourse note, bringing the total basis to $25,000. Under rules in effect before 1986, the investor's basis was $25,000; under the new rules, the nonrecourse loan is not included for the purposes of computing a tax loss. Benefits apply only to $10,000 or 40 percent of losses generated in the program.

Such an investment is also classified as a passive activity. Even when losses do occur, they can be deducted only to the extent that they offset passive income in the same year. In order to claim a loss, your investment basis must be "at-risk." The amount considered at-risk includes the following:

1. Cash actually invested.
2. Recourse loans, financing that you are liable to repay or that is fully secured by a pledge of other property.

Simply being required to pay back a loan does not always qualify it as at-risk. Part of your basis in an investment will also be excluded from the deductibility rule if the lender is a fellow investor or is related to an investor in the program, or if the loan contract includes clauses protecting the borrower against loss (by way of guarantees, stop-loss clauses, insurance, or the right to convert the loan to nonrecourse status).

With the combination of passive loss limitation rules, a ceiling on deductibility of investment interest, and the at-risk restriction, the tax shelter industry has been effectively shut down. Today, limited partnerships must emphasize economic benefits instead of tax benefits in order to attract investment capital. Rather than offer manufactured tax losses, programs must now promise a real net income to investors.

However, tax sheltering is still possible. For example, a partnership reporting income to investors continues to provide a degree of shelter through depreciation, and properties purchased in the program have the potential for increased market value. You may earn a cash profit and have part of that profit protected from taxes.

> *Example:* You own units in a real estate limited partnership. This year, your portion of cash flow was $1,200. However, you were also entitled to $400 in depreciation on the property held by the

program. Only $800 of your cash income is taxed as net investment income.

Passive income is also sheltered when passive losses are applied against it. Those losses may occur during the same year or may be held over from a previous year.

Example: This year, you are liable for taxes on $6,500 in passive income from a limited partnership. However, you have carried over $4,000 from previous years in unused passive losses. When these losses are applied against current-year income, the net result is taxable income of $2,500.

Tax-Exempt Bonds

Virtually the only remaining tax-exempt investment is the municipal bond. Provisions of the Tax Reform Act of 1986 have curtailed the exempt status of some bonds, but others continue to be exempt from federal tax.

Two Supreme Court cases established the rule that the federal government may not tax income from state and local debt: *McCullock vs. Maryland* (1819) and *Pollock vs. Farmer's Loan and Trust Company* (1895). Both of these decisions were made well before passage of the first permanent income tax law in 1913, and the exemption from federal taxes of all municipal bonds was the rule—until 1986. *Municipal bonds*—those debt securities issued by state or local governments and their agencies—are now divided into four groups:

1. *Public purpose bonds.* Interest on these bonds is fully exempt from federal taxes. Included are bonds issued to fund essential activities of the municipality, such as highways and schools. The full deductibility of a municipal bond is an attractive feature; however, it also means that the yield will be lower than on a similar, taxable bond.
2. *Nongovernmental purpose bonds.* Interest on these bonds is issued to finance activities not directly related to a public purpose, such as student loans or housing projects, and it *might* be free from tax. A municipality is subject to a cap on the amount of nongovernmental purpose bonds it may issue. Above that cap, interest becomes taxable at the federal level. Interest on all bonds in this group is treated as a preference item, meaning that investors are subject to the alternative minimum tax (see Chapter 14).

3. *Private activity bonds.* Any bond issued to finance nonessential activities is subject to federal income tax. This includes bonds issued to pay for projects like sports arenas, shopping malls, and loans to farmers.
4. *Bonds issued before August 7, 1986.* Bonds existing and outstanding before the date the rules changed are still taxed under the old system. They are entirely exempt from federal tax, regardless of their classification.

In addition to being exempt from federal taxes, a public purpose municipal bond is often free of tax at the state and local level as well. This could translate to a tremendous benefit to investors paying both taxes.

> *Example:* You invest in a fully tax-exempt municipal bond. Your federal rate is 33 percent, and your state income tax rate is an additional 8 percent. The double exemption feature makes municipal bonds attractive compared with taxable bonds.

Comparing the Yield

Before buying fully exempt municipal bonds, you should always compute the *equivalent yield,* which is the taxable yield you would need to match the bond's interest. This shows whether or not it is worth seeking tax-exempt income. Even if the tax-exempt bond is yielding less than a taxable bond, it may still be a better after-tax investment, if the taxable bond has an unacceptable risk.

You also need to ensure that the comparison is valid in terms of risk. The bonds being compared should have a similar safety rating assigned by one or more of the bond rating services (Fitch, Moody's, or Standard and Poor's). Bonds with ratings between AAA and BBB are considered investment grade. Any rating lower than this range is speculative in varying degrees.

> *Example:* An investor is comparing yields on a municipal bond rated AA and a speculative corporate bond yielding a much higher annual rate but with a rate of C. Because the safety ratings are so different, the comparison is not valid.

The formula for finding equivalent yield is shown in Figure 13-1.

$$\frac{T}{100 - B} = E$$

T = tax–exempt yield
B = tax bracket
E = equivalent yield

FIGURE 13-1 Formula: Equivalent Yield

Example: Your tax rate this year is 33 percent, so you will be taxed at that rate for any investment income earned between now and the end of the year. You are considering purchasing a tax-exempt municipal bond yielding 6.50 percent, or you could purchase a taxable corporate bond with a similar safety rating but yielding 9.25 percent. Is the municipal bond a better investment? To find out, you apply the formula:

$$\frac{6.5\%}{100 - 33} = 9.70\%$$

In this case, the municipal bond offers a better yield. The rate is higher *on an equivalent basis* than the rate offered on the taxable bond because you

ACTION CHECKLIST

Tax-Exempt Investments

1. Become familiar with the rules for taxation of the following:
   a. Public purpose bonds.
   b. Nongovernmental purpose bonds.
   c. Private activity bonds.
   d. Bonds issued before August 7, 1986.
2. Compare tax-exempt income to after-tax yields on taxable bonds.
3. Ensure that risk levels are approximately the same for bonds you are comparing, in terms of the company's financial strength and collateral, and the bond's time to maturity.

would need to earn a taxable yield of 9.70 percent to match the yield on the municipal bond:

Taxable yield	9.70%
Less tax, 33%	3.20
After-tax yield	6.50%

The required after-tax yield will be higher if you are also liable for state and local taxes. The higher your overall tax liability, the more likely that a tax-exempt bond will yield a higher after-tax return.

Comparing Risks

You should never take on an investment without first knowing the risks involved. They should be acceptable to your personal plan and suitable for the goals you have set. Additionally, features like tax exemption should not be the sole factor considered in your selection.

Bond investments involve market risk. For example, if the rate you earn today is lower than the rates available on bonds in the future, the market appeal of your bond will fall. The market value, as a consequence, will be discounted. Of course, risk is also an opportunity. For example, if the rate you lock in today is relatively high compared with future market rates, then your bond's market value will gain a premium.

When bonds are discounted well below par value, you could also face liquidity risk: It will be impossible to close out your investment without also accepting a loss.

Example: A $5,000 municipal bond has been discounted to 94 (meaning 94 percent of face value), so your investment has a current market value of $4,700. You can sell the bond, but only if you are willing to accept a loss of $300.

Bonds are also subject to *default risk.* An issuer could be late in making scheduled interest payments or default on the principal amount. Many investors consider default a remote possibility, as evidenced by the popularity during the 1980s of junk bonds, which are bonds with safety ratings below investment grade. However, default is a real possibility for all but the highest-quality bonds.

Overemphasis in any one market is also a risk. Diversification is an important, basic principle worth following even when selecting very safe, secure products. Avoid placing too high a portion of your total investment capital in any one classification.

One final risk is inaccurate comparison. Whenever you are deciding between two different investments, make sure the criteria are similar. For example, do not compare two bonds with different safety ratings. The yields on each bond are not the only means for judging investment potential: Yield reflects market conditions, tax status, and safety. Bonds that are more speculative will yield more, but they might also be inappropriate for the goals you have set and for your personal investment and risk standards.

> *Example:* You are setting up an investment program for your child's college education. You will need to cash in your portfolio for this purpose in 12 years, so you are reviewing bonds that will mature at that time. You have calculated that to reach the target amount you need an annual yield of 6 percent or more. One low-rated bond is currently yielding 9.2 percent. This is not appropriate for two reasons: First, you do not need to have a yield at that level. Second, the risk is too great, considering the goal itself.

In setting goals, you will establish the appropriate degree of risk for yourself. When saving for a child's college education, for example, you are more likely to seek relatively secure investments and to avoid excessive risk and speculation.

Specific goals help you to establish a personal investment policy that is defined by risk tolerance. How much risk is appropriate? What investments fit that tolerance level? And how should different investments within the acceptable range be compared? These questions help you to set standards for yourself.

The tax-exempt status of some municipal bonds should not be the sole basis for making an investment decision. In certain instances, a diversified portfolio will include tax-exempt municipal bonds, but in others there is simply no need to include them. When the equivalent yield of taxable investments is better, for example, investing just to avoid taxes makes no sense. You are better off paying taxes on the taxable bond and ending up with a higher after-tax yield.

Methods of Buying

At the time they are first issued, municipal bonds can be purchased directly from the brokerage firms acting with the underwriter (the company that takes the bond issue to the market). Existing bonds can also be purchased at the current market price from a brokerage firm at any time after they are issued and before they mature. That price varies according to safety ratings and the rate of interest, in comparison with the rates offered on other bonds on the market.

For many investors, direct purchase of municipal bonds requires too much capital or involves a high transaction fee. In those instances, you can achieve diversification by buying shares in *bond mutual funds.* A tax-exempt bond fund is designed to purchase only municipal bonds on which there is no federal tax. This is one of the few ways to achieve a compounded rate of return on a debt security investment. By instructing the fund's management to reinvest interest, you will earn more than when you have it paid out to you. A distinction should be made, though, between tax-exempt interest and taxable capital gains. Any capital gains earned in a fund are taxable.

> *Example:* You have purchased shares in a tax-exempt bond fund. This year, the fund sold several bonds and made a profit based on changes in market value. That portion of income, classified as a capital gain, is taxable. Interest continues to be tax-exempt.

You can also invest in a tax-exempt money market fund. These funds invest in short-term, public purpose debt securities of municipalities and their agencies. They are designed to provide tax-exempt income on money market instruments rather than on longer-term bonds.

A third pool is the tax-exempt unit investment trust (UITs were discussed in Chapter 9). The trust purchases a fixed portfolio of bonds and pays interest and return of principle on a schedule. Return of principle occurs when the bonds mature, and the trust will not sell bonds before that date. You know well in advance when payments will come to you. The disadvantage of the UIT is that it is not managed. When a bond's rating is changed, for example, the trust does not make a decision to sell (except in extreme cases). In comparison, a bond mutual fund cannot guarantee future payment levels, but it does manage its investment portfolio.

The range of available tax-exempt investments is very limited under current tax rules. These products are appropriate for some portfolios but not for all. Even when you buy tax-advantaged products, you could be subject to the alternative minimum tax. The rule for this tax are covered in the next chapter.

CHAPTER 14

The Alternative Minimum Tax

The complexities in federal tax law are designed to set rules for every possible form of income and deduction. As a consequence, loopholes have been created, and in the past so many existed that it was possible to avoid taxes on large blocks of income. People in higher tax brackets could take advantage of this situation by using investment capital to create certain types of losses and deductions, by timing losses in programs, and by deferring taxes using many tax shelter provisions. The tax burden was carried primarily by middle-income taxpayers.

Congress took two major steps to change this situation. First, it enacted new laws to eliminate abusive tax shelters by restricting deductions for passive losses and investment interest. Second, it created the *alternative minimum tax (AMT)* to ensure that most people would be liable for some tax each year.

The first version of the AMT took effect in January, 1979. The rules were expanded under the terms of the Tax Equity and Fiscal Responsibility Act of 1982 (TEFRA), which was enacted on August 19, 1982, and they were modified again with the passage of the Tax Reform Act of 1986.

AMT Rules

Under current law, the alternative minimum tax applies when you report certain types of income or loss (explained shortly) or when you claim

TABLE 14-1 The AMT Exemption

	MAXIMUM EXEMPTION	LESS 25% OF AMTI
Single	$30,000	$112,500
Married, filing joint return	$40,000	$150,000
Married, filing separately; estate or trust	$20,000	$ 75,000

some types of itemized deductions. It requires a second computation beyond the regular one, with many of the rules changed. If the total tax liability under the AMT calculation is higher, you are liable for an additional tax. The second calculation is specific, and will be described later.

The current AMT rate is 21 percent, an increase over the past rate of 20 percent. Although this is lower than the regular tax brackets of 28 and 33 percent, certain preference items must be added in, and a number of itemized deductions allowed under the regular method are excluded. *Preference items* are deductions, losses, and certain allowances that are reduced or disallowed for AMT purposes.

Under the rules, you begin with taxable income as reported under the regular method; then you add preference income and disallowed itemized deductions; finally, you subtract your exemption. The exemption is based on your reporting status and *alternative minimum tax income (AMTI)*. Single people are allowed an exemption of $30,000; if you are married and file a joint return, the exemption is $40,000; and for married people filing separately or estates and trusts, the exemption is $20,000. However, the exemption begins to be reduced when income exceeds specified levels, and it is phased out completely by the time income reaches certain amounts. Table 14-1 describes the formula used. The exemption is phased out once your income passes a specified level. Thus, for single people, no exemption is available when their alternative minimum tax income reaches $232,500—that is, when the formula produces an amount ($30,000) that equals the exemption allowed:

Total AMTI	$232,500
Less phase-out level	112,500
Difference	$120,000
25%	$ 30,000

For married couples filing joint returns, the exemption is phased out when AMTI reaches $310,000:

Total AMTI	$310,000
Less phase-out level	150,000
Difference	$160,000
25%	$ 40,000

And for married people filing separately and for estates or trusts, the exemption disappears at or above $155,000:

Total AMTI	$155,000
Less: phase-out level	75,000
Difference	$ 80,000
25%	$ 20,000

No tax credits are allowed under alternative minimum tax rules, except one: a foreign tax credit. This applies only if you are liable for taxes in a foreign country.

Depreciation Rules

In 1981, a new tax law changed the methods for computing depreciation. The Economic Recovery Tax Act (ERTA) introduced the *accelerated cost recovery system*, or *ACRS*. It established *recovery periods* (the time required to fully depreciate an asset) for each type of depreciable asset, and it allowed some elections to use straight-line methods in place of accelerated depreciation. This simplified the depreciation rules in one respect: There are now fewer choices to make when an asset is purchased, because it fits into a specific category and is subject to the rules of that category. For example, some classes of assets may be depreciated under an accelerated method; you may also make an election to apply straight-line depreciation or even to extend the recovery period. The ACRS rules also replaced the older concept dictating that assets were to be assigned a salvage value, which could not be depreciated. Salvage value was an amount of left-over value that could not be depreciated. Since 1981, the rules have been changed again. As part of the Tax Reform Act of 1986, depreciation on business and investment assets is computed under the *modified accelerated cost recovery system (MACRS)*. This system applies to all assets placed into service after December 31, 1986. According to the MACRS, each asset is depreciated on the basis of its recovery period and the month it was placed into service. During the first year, a percentage of the basis is claimed based on the month purchased. Table 14-2 summarizes the rules

TABLE 14-2 Depreciation, Residential Property

MONTH PLACED IN SERVICE	Year			
	1	2–27	28	29
1	3.48%	3.64%	1.88%	
2	3.18	3.64	2.18	
3	2.88	3.64	2.48	
4	2.58	3.64	2.78	
5	2.27	3.64	3.09	
6	1.97	3.64	3.39	
7	1.67	3.64	3.64	0.05%
8	1.36	3.64	3.64	0.36
9	1.06	3.64	3.64	0.66
10	0.76	3.64	3.64	0.96
11	0.45	3.64	3.64	1.27
12	0.15	3.64	3.64	1.57

for residential real estate, which is depreciated over 27.5 years using the straight-line method. The percentages for each month tell you the percentage of the asset's depreciable value that can be claimed each year.

Example: You own a rental home for which you paid $150,000. The value of the land is $25,000, so you are allowed to claim depreciation on $125,000. You will use the straight-line method, over 27.5 years. Refer to Table 14-2 for the following two illustrations:

A: The home was placed in service in May.

YEAR(S)	%	AMOUNT
1	2.27%	$2,837.50
2–27	3.64	$4,550.00
28	3.09	$3,862.50

Total depreciation:

Year 1	$ 2,837.50
Years 2–27 ($4,550 × 26)	118,300.00
Year 28	3,862.50
Total	$125,000.00

B: *The home was placed in service in November.*

YEAR(S)	%	AMOUNT
1	0.45%	$ 562.50
2–27	3.64	$4,550.00
28	3.64	$4,550.00
29	1.27	$1,587.50

Total depreciation:

Year 1	$ 562.50
Years 2–27 ($4,550 × 26)	118,300.00
Year 28	4,550.00
Year 29	1,587.50
Total	$125,000.00

Nonresidential property is subject to straight-line depreciation over 31.5 years. Table 14-3 shows the applicable annual percentages allowed, based on the month the property is placed into service.

TABLE 14-3 Depreciation, Nonresidential Property

MONTH PLACED IN SERVICE	Year			
	1	2–27	28	29
1	3.04%	3.17%	1.86%	
2	2.78	3.17	2.12	
3	2.51	3.17	2.39	
4	2.25	3.17	2.65	
5	1.98	3.17	2.92	
6	1.72	3.17	3.17	
7	1.46	3.17	3.17	0.27%
8	1.19	3.17	3.17	0.54
9	0.93	3.17	3.17	0.80
10	0.66	3.17	3.17	1.07
11	0.40	3.17	3.17	1.33
12	0.13	3.17	3.17	1.60

AMT Depreciation

Under the alternative minimum tax, passive gain or loss is computed separately from deductions for depreciation. Thus, a net loss could consist of several parts: an operating gain offset by a separate amount for depreciation, or a separation of a net loss into two distinct parts.

> *Example:* This year you have a passive loss from a real estate limited partnership. The total loss includes interest and depreciation, offset by a net operating gain. In this case, the computations of income, interest, and depreciation are separated when computing alternative minimum tax.

The recomputed depreciation on investment and business assets applies only for the purpose of the alternative minimum tax. If you are not liable for this tax, you will continue to claim depreciation under the prevailing rules. However, all those who most compute AMT every year must keep two sets of depreciation records: one for the regular tax, and one for the alternative minimum tax. The rules for the AMT on real and personal property are discussed in the following paragraphs.

Depreciation on Real Property

You are required to use straight-line depreciation on real estate. As already explained, under the regular method, residential property is depreciated over 27.5 years, and commercial property is depreciated over 31.5 years. Under AMT rules, the computation is done over 40 years, so the amount of depreciation you can claim is reduced.

> *Example:* Several years ago, you purchased a home for investment purposes at a cost of $150,000. Land, which is not depreciable, is worth $25,000, and the building's basis is therefore $125,000. Annual depreciation under the regular method and under AMT rules is as follows:

27.5 years	$4,545
40 years	3,125
Preference amount	$1,420

The difference between the two computations, $1,420, is considered the *preference amount*. This is added back to taxable income for the AMT computation and is subject to the AMT tax at the rate of 21 percent, if that tax is greater than tax computed under the regular method.

Depreciation on Personal Property

Under the regular method, many types of personal property are depreciated under the *200 percent declining-balance method*. To compute, first figure the straight-line amount; then multiply that by 200 percent. The base is reduced each year by the amount of depreciation claimed previously. As a result, more depreciation is claimed in the early years, and less later on.

Under AMT rules, you may still use the declining-balance method, but only at the rate of 150 percent.

Example: You have purchased personal property for $8,000, which is used as part of your investment in real estate. It is depreciated over a five-year recovery period under the regular rules, using the 200 percent declining-balance method. However, you are also liable for the alternative minimum tax, so you are restricted to the 150 percent method. Depreciation on this property must be recalculated and the difference treated as a preference amount:

$$200\% \text{ method:}$$
$$\frac{\$8,000}{5} \times 200\% = \$3,200$$

$$150\% \text{ method:}$$
$$\frac{\$8,000}{5} \times 150\% = \underline{\$2,400}$$

Preference
amount: $\underline{\$\ \ 800}$

This amount must be added back to income and is subject to the alternative minimum tax.

Netting of Depreciation

Under the regular method, depreciation is accelerated during the early years and declines in later years. When AMT depreciation is used in place of the regular method, the period is extended. This means that, in the later years, the AMT computation may produce a *higher* allowance than the regular method.

You are not allowed to deduct a negative preference when depreciation is calculated on an asset-to-asset basis. For example, if MACRS depreciation is $2,000 and depreciation under the AMT calculation is $2,400, there will be no preference amount.

However, you are allowed to add all assets together and to report the net preference amount. This *netting* eliminates the negative preferences that will eventually show up on assets held for a longer period of time.

Example: You compute AMT depreciation on three investment assets this year. They are netted together:

ASSET	MACRS	AMT	PREFERENCE AMOUNT
1	$ 6,000	$3,600	$2,400
2	3,500	2,625	875
3	2,000	2,400	(400)
Total	$11,500	$8,625	$2,875

If each asset's AMT depreciation had been computed separately, no preference amount would have applied to asset number 3, because it is negative. The preference amount would have been $3,275 (differences on assets 1 and 2 only).

Pre-1987 Rules

Before the Tax Reform Act of 1986 went into effect, you were allowed to claim depreciation on real estate using accelerated methods. In addition, real property could be depreciated over a period as short as 19 years. If you own property purchased and placed into service before 1987, the AMT calculation removes the accelerated depreciation benefits.

The preference amount, in these cases, is the difference between the depreciation allowed under the 19-year accelerated method and depreciation calculated on a straight-line basis. In the earlier years, this will create a preference amount; in the later years, when straight-line will be higher, there will be no preference amount. In those cases, the negative preference can be netted against other preference amounts.

Table 14-4 summarizes the percentage of total basis that can be claimed each year under pre-1987 rules, based on the month the prop-

TABLE 14-4 Pre-1987 Depreciation, Accelerated 19-Year
Recovery Period

MONTH PLACED IN SERVICE	Year					
	1	2	3	4	5	6
1	8.8%	8.4%	7.6%	6.9%	6.3%	5.7%
2	8.1	8.5	7.7	7.0	6.3	5.7
3	7.3	8.5	7.7	7.0	6.4	5.8
4	6.5	8.6	7.8	7.1	6.4	5.9
5	5.8	8.7	7.9	7.1	6.5	5.9
6	5.0	8.8	7.9	7.2	6.5	5.9
7	4.2	8.8	8.0	7.3	6.6	6.0
8	3.5	8.9	8.1	7.3	6.6	6.0
9	2.7	9.0	8.1	7.4	6.7	6.1
10	1.9	9.0	8.2	7.4	6.8	6.1
11	1.1	9.1	8.3	7.5	6.8	6.2
12	0.4	9.2	8.3	7.6	6.9	6.2

MONTH PLACED IN SERVICE	Year				
	7	8	9	10–19	20
1	5.2%	4.7%	4.2%	4.2%	0.2%
2	5.2	4.7	4.3	4.2	0.5
3	5.3	4.8	4.3	4.2	0.9
4	5.3	4.8	4.4	4.2	1.2
5	5.3	4.8	4.4	4.2	1.6
6	5.4	4.9	4.5	4.2	1.9
7	5.4	4.9	4.5	4.2	2.3
8	5.5	5.0	4.5	4.2	2.6
9	5.5	5.0	4.5	4.2	3.0
10	5.6	5.1	4.6	4.2	3.3
11	5.6	5.1	4.6	4.2	3.7
12	5.6	5.1	4.7	4.2	4.0

erty was originally placed in service. Note that the percentage declines over the first nine years (the accelerated depreciation period) and then reverts to straight-line for the remainder of the period.

In computing the preference amount for the alternative minimum tax, you compare the percentages allowed under the old rules with the straight-line depreciation allowance shown in Table 14-5. If you are re-

TABLE 14-5 Pre-1987 Depreciation, Straight-Line 19-Year Recovery Period

MONTH PLACED IN SERVICE	Year			
	1	2–13	14–19	20
1	5.0%	5.3%	5.2%	0.2%
2	4.6	5.3	5.2	0.6
3	4.2	5.3	5.2	1.0
4	3.7	5.3	5.2	1.5
5	3.3	5.3	5.2	1.9
6	2.9	5.3	5.2	2.3
7	2.4	5.3	5.2	2.8
8	2.0	5.3	5.2	3.2
9	1.5	5.3	5.2	3.7
10	1.1	5.3	5.2	4.1
11	0.7	5.3	5.2	4.5
12	0.2	5.3	5.2	5.0

porting claimed depreciation on real property purchased before 1987 and you are using 19-year accelerated depreciation, a recalculation will be necessary—if you are liable for the alternative minimum tax.

Example: You purchased investment property in October, 1985 for $150,000. Land was originally valued at $25,000, so the balance of $125,000 is subject to depreciation. You have been using the 19-year recovery period and accelerated depreciation under pre-1987 rules. In 1992, the seventh year, 5.6 percent, or $7,000, was allowed under the old rules. (Refer to Table 14-4, line 10, for the 10th month, and the column for the 7th year.) In 1992, you were liable for the alternative minimum tax, so depreciation had to be recalculated. Refer to Table 14-5, the 10th line and the column for years 2 through 13. You were allowed 5.3 percent under the recalculation for the alternative minimum tax:

Pre-1987 allowance:		
$125,000 × 5.6%	=	$7,000
AMT recalculation:		
$125,000 × 5.3%	=	$6,625
Preference amount:		$ 375

In this case, you were required to add $375 as a preference amount to calculate your AMT.

The AMT rules for personal property apply only if you lease that property to someone else. You are then required to use straight-line depreciation *and* to recalculate over a longer recovery period.

Example: You own furniture, which you provide to tenants in rental properties you own, under a separate leasing agreement. The preference amount will be the excess of accelerated depreciation over a calculated straight-line depreciation; it will also be calculated for an extended recovery period:

ACRS YEARS	AMT YEARS
3	5
5	8
10	15
15	22

The preference amount will consist of both factors: the loss of accelerated depreciation and a smaller allowance due to the extended recovery period.

Other Preference Items

Many types of income are treated as preference items for the AMT calculation. The rules disallow deferral or calculation of appreciated basis in property. Of special interest to investors are the following groups.

Incentive Stock Options

Stock options may be given to employees as a form of deferred compensation. The option is granted at current market value but is not taxed as income at the time. Stock can be purchased whenever the employee wishes.

Example: Your employer gives you an option for 100 shares of stock at the current market price of $35 per share. A year later, the stock's value has risen to $50 per share. You exercise your option, purchasing at the option price, and pay $3,500. Under the regular rule, you are taxed only when you sell the stock. However, under AMT, the difference between the option price and the current market value is taxed as a preference amount. In this instance, that is $1,500 (current value of $50 less option price of $35, or $15 per share).

Charitable Donations

In the past, one popular loophole involved purchasing property at a relatively low value, having it appraised at a much higher level, and then donating it at the appraised value. In the highest tax brackets, this could produce a tax benefit greater than the investment amount. For example, an investor paying tax in the 50 percent bracket could purchase an asset for $10,000 and then have it appraised for $30,000. By donating that property and writing off the $30,000, the investor could reduce taxes by $15,000.

That loophole was closed by rules for any transaction entered for obvious tax benefits. But the alternative minimum tax also applies in such cases, even when no abusive motive is involved. You may donate property and claim a deduction based on current market value, but that may also qualify you for AMT.

Example: You have owned real estate for many years, and you donated it this year to a charity. At the time title was transferred, the property was appraised at $215,000. Your basis was $65,000. The difference, $150,000, cannot be counted as an itemized deduction; it is considered a preference amount.

Installment Sales

With property sold under the installment method, you are allowed to defer part of the taxable gain until future years. An installment sale occurs in stages over a number of years. Under terms of the Tax Reform Act of 1986, deferral is completely disallowed for the alternative minimum tax if the real property is sold for $150,000 or more.

Example: You sold property last year for $215,000 using the installment sales method. Your taxable profit was $150,000, and you will receive one-fifth of the total sales price per year for five years. Using the regular method, taxable income on the $150,000 profit would have been reported as $30,000 per year. However, under

A C T I O N   C H E C K L I S T

Alternative Minimum Tax

1. Learn the rules of the alternative minimum tax as
   they apply this year.
2. Seek professional help if you are subject to the alternative minimum tax.
3. Modify your plan to anticipate and manage the effects
   of AMT.
4. Learn how to estimate AMT and use that calculation
   as a tax-planning tool.

---

the alternative minimum tax rules, the entire profit of $150,000 is counted during the year of the sale.

Miscellaneous Items

If you are liable for the AMT, some itemized deductions allowed under the regular method must be added back as preference amounts. These include state and local income taxes (offset by an exclusion for any tax refunds reported as income during the year), real estate and other taxes, and miscellaneous itemized deductions.

You are allowed to claim casualty and theft losses, gambling losses (but only to the extent that they offset gambling winnings), charitable donations, medical deductions above 10 percent of adjusted gross income (under the regular method, medical expenses are allowed above 7.5 percent), mortgage interest on loans to purchase or rehabilitate a primary or secondary residence, and net investment interest. Interest on mortgage loans above your basis in property (cost plus improvements) cannot be deducted.

An AMT Example

After calculating your taxable income under AMT rules, you are allowed to reduce that amount by the exemption.

> *Example:* A married couple is allowed a maximum exemption from AMT of $40,000. That exemption is reduced by 25 percent of AMTI over $150,000. Their AMTI this year is $241,817:

Maximum exemption		$40,000
AMTI	$241,817	
Phase-out level	150,000	
Excess	$ 91,817	
	× 25%	
Reduction		22,954
Exemption allowed		$17,046

Figure 14-1a is a worksheet for computing the alternative minimum tax, and a filled-in example is shown in Figure 14-1b.

A	taxable income	$_____
B	plus: adjustments for itemized deductions	
	_____	_____
	_____	_____
	_____	_____
C	plus: tax preference items	
	_____	_____
	_____	_____
	_____	_____
D	total ALTI (A + B + C)	$_____
E	maximum exemption	$_____
F	phaseout amount	$_____
G	net (D − F)	_____
H	exclusion (G x 25%)	_____
I	exemption (E − H)	_____
J	taxable amount (D − I)	$_____
K	tax (J x 21%)	$_____
L	regular tax liability	_____
M	alternative minimum tax (K − L)	$_____

FIGURE 14-1a Worksheet: Alternative Minimum Tax

A	taxable income	$ 132,400
B	plus: adjustments for itemized deductions	
	taxes	11,800
	interest	1,217
C	plus: tax preference items accelerated depreciation	2,400
	appreciated value, charitable donation	94,000
D	total ALTI (A + B + C)	$241,817
E	maximum exemption	$ 40,000
F	phaseout amount	$150,000
G	net (D − F)	91,817
H	exclusion (G x 25%)	22,954
I	exemption (E − H)	17,046
J	taxable amount (D − I)	$224,771
K	tax (J x 21%)	$ 47,202
L	regular tax liability	35,926
M	alternative minimum tax (K − L)	$ 11,276

FIGURE 14-1b Worksheet: Alternative Minimum Tax

The actual AMT calculation is completed on IRS form 6251. You can order this form and instructions by calling the IRS forms ordering number in your area.

The alternative minimum tax is a complication that requires many people to compute their tax in two ways rather than in one. These complications and other tax rules make it essential to plan and develop ideas for legal tax avoidance and deferral. Investment planning as a year-round strategy is an important part of the process, and you also need to develop a simple but complete system for keeping records of your transactions. These topics are explained in the next chapter.

CHAPTER 15

Tax Rules of Thumb

Reaching your investment goals depends on setting and following rules—for selecting products, for timing your purchase or sale, and for diversifying your portfolio. The process should be tied to goals, and you need to be constantly aware of risk.

In addition to these basic rules, you also need to know of the tax benefits or consequences of the products you select. The timing and status of income or loss derived from your investment activity could make a difference between profit and loss in any one year. In some cases, the tax outcome may be more important than the pre-tax profit. This is not to suggest that the tax motive should ever be more important than the economic; however, you do need to be aware of how your profits will be affected by taxes at the end of the year.

Methods of Taxation

The rules for federal taxation are the result of attempts to equally distribute the tax burden. At the same time, however, taxation works as an economic and political force. When tax rules do not favor investment in assets, there is a direct consequence in the economy; and when big business is given too many tax breaks, individuals complain that they are carrying an unfair share of the burden.

The number of newly developed tax laws during the 1980s affected investors very directly. As already discussed, restrictions on tax-motivated shelters erased the major loopholes that had existed before. The Tax Reform Act of 1986 changed the entire structure of taxation by introducing the three-bracket system. That means there are only three tax rates. At the same time, a number of deductions were taken away or severely restricted. For a number of people, this legislation was, in effect, a tax increase.

Debate has been under way for a number of years concerning the best method for taxing earnings. A flat tax has been proposed as more equitable; changes in the progressive bracketing system is yet another alternative. Some have suggested replacing the taxation of income with a national sales tax. With the national debt a chronic problem, a sales tax may eventually become reality, not as a replacement but as an additional tax.

You may be certain that the tax rules will change again in the future. The trend is moving toward fewer deductions and advantages, the possibility of higher brackets (a tax increase), and the elimination of special rules in many areas. The many ways in which you can defer taxes today may be reduced in the future as well. One example of this has occurred already. The alternative minimum tax, in many respects, assesses a current tax on certain transactions that are otherwise deferred.

As long as income is taxed, earning a profit comes with a penalty. Part of that profit will be given to the government. So the more profitable your investment activity, the higher your share of the tax burden will become.

Avoidance Strategies

Tax planning and avoidance are legal strategies. Every investor may employ planning techniques to minimize the current year's tax burden, which has made deferral a popular and widely practiced idea.

As part of your investment strategy, employ ideas to look for timing opportunities. The following are some guidelines for developing your own tax-planning program:

1. *Remember, timing is the key.* If you want to reduce your taxes this year, timing your actions makes all the difference. A number of transactions, properly timed, will reduce your tax burden.

   Some examples include depositing funds in an IRA or Keogh

account, opening the deferral account by the deadline, and timing the sale of an investment you are holding at a loss position.

Example: You have $13,000 in reportable capital gains this year. In January, you begin to review your tax status for the year just ended to get an idea of how much liability you have. You own stocks that have declined in value, and you would be willing to sell them and take your loss now to offset the gains. However, that action will have to be taken before December 31. By January, it will be too late.

2. *Your planning strategy should be merged with your investment strategy.* Tax-planning strategy and investment strategy cannot be separated; they belong together. If you apply tax-planning techniques as part of the process of managing your portfolio and not as an unrelated routine, you have a better chance of avoiding taxes each year or of deferring a liability until the future.

Example: You earned profits this year in excess of $5,000. You are not qualified to write off contributions to an IRA account, so your investments were made without the deferral feature: By qualified, we mean the rules allow or disallow you to claim a deduction. However, your strategy is to not use investment capital until retirement. Given that goal, it would make sense to shift $2,000 per year in funds to an IRA account, where profits are not taxed until funds are withdrawn.

3. *Planning should be a year-round process.* Year-end planning is valuable but limited. To really manage your tax status, you need to review your status throughout the year. A quarterly review can help you to plan far in advance.

Example: You expect to earn substantial profits from investments this year. Your employer withholds taxes from your paycheck, but you suspect that the amount will be far below your liability. You begin reviewing your tax status at the end of each quarter. One purpose is to look for ways to defer liabilities; another is to estimate the year's tax burden in case you are liable for quarterly prepayments.

Remember your investment motive as the primary guideline for your decisions. Avoid the mistake of taking action to reduce taxes when that action is contrary to your goals. Most investors want to accumulate capital in products suitable for their own purposes. If you borrow money to invest, for example, you need to ensure that the profits you earn are greater than the cost of borrowing.

Example: One investor sold stocks early in the year and wanted to find write-offs to reduce taxes. He refinanced his home to free up investment capital, with the idea of creating higher interest expenses. Although this did create a large itemized deduction, it was contrary to the profit motive. The total interest deduction for the year was $7,000. That produced a tax benefit of $2,310 (33 percent); however, the after-tax cost of borrowing money was still $4,690. In this case, the tax motive distracted the investor from his real goal.

Another mistake worth avoiding is deferring profits you should take now, because of a tax motive. For example, in the stock market, you may reach your predetermined goal and delay selling because you are worried about taxes. Stick to the goal. Deal with the tax consequence as a secondary problem, and do not let your profits slip away.

One alternative to selling in the current year is to protect the stock's market position by using options as a form of insurance. As discussed in Chapter 9, a put option protects a stock's current market value. If that value declines, the put option's value will rise point for point to offset the loss. The cost of buying a put can be thought of as a form of insurance against the risk of declining market value. If the stock does fall in value, the put can be exercised (allowing you to sell 100 shares at the set value) or the put can be sold at a profit—offsetting the loss in the stock's value.

A third mistake is to position yourself in a deferred investment or account when that is contrary to your goals. Deferral is appropriate for long-term goals but not for situations in which you will need to get your money back in the near future.

Example: A married couple wanted to set up an emergency reserve fund equal to three months' net salary. They considered placing funds in a money market account but instead decided to purchase a tax-deferred annuity, reasoning that income taxes would be deferred with the annuity. But this also meant that they could only get their emergency funds by paying a penalty for every withdrawal, both to the insurance company and in taxes. Thus they overlooked the purpose of the funds: to provide money needed for emergencies, meaning immediate availability.

A C T I O N   C H E C K L I S T

Tax Planning

1. Hire a professional tax adviser who is familiar with current rules for investors.
2. For proper tax planning, begin the process of periodic review.
3. Seek avoidance strategies to defer tax liabilities to the future. Merge timing and investment strategies.
4. Never hesitate to take a profit because of tax motives. Always let the profit motive rule. Overcome belief in the myth that profits should be avoided if they will be taxed. That makes no sense at all.

The Dangers of Leverage

As the previews discussion makes clear, it is critical to keep in mind that you are better off earning a large profit this year and paying taxes than you are making no profit. Tax reduction often becomes an obsessive pseudo-goal and prevents people from remembering *why* they invest money. The leveraged strategy is a perfect example of this obsession. It pays to check the numbers before going into debt to create investment capital. The following are some points to consider about leveraged investing:

1. *If the interest rate you pay is higher than the amount you earn, that defeats the purpose.* Some market "wisdom" states that smart investors know how to put money to work. That means going into debt to free up money and taking advantage of profitable opportunities. A well-managed program that includes leverage can have that result; however, when you have to pay back a debt, you have two problems. First, you need the cash flow to afford regular payments. Second, the profit you earn will be reduced by interest payments. In some cases, you will lose more in interest than you earn from your investments.
2. *Interest reduces total return without also reducing the risks associated with the investment.* The risk factor is too easily overlooked when you leverage your capital. You might find an investment opportunity and not have funds available, so you borrow money. However, how much risk is involved with the investment? Are you willing to take that risk with borrowed money? No matter what

happens in the investment, you will still be responsible for repaying the loan.

There may be other forms of risk. How safe is your capital? The investment may offer the potential for a very high rate of return, but that could also mean you risk losing part of your capital as well. Can you afford the risk? Is it worthwhile with borrowed money?

3. *The tax benefit of writing off interest is only one side of the issue.* Anyone who encourages you to borrow money to invest probably emphasizes the tax benefits of writing off the interest, especially if you finance the investment with a home mortgage. The argument often goes like this: "You will earn 8 percent on this investment. Although your interest is 10 percent, you also get the tax deduction of 33 percent, so your after-tax interest will be only 6.7 percent, well below what you will earn." The flaw in this argument is that the 8 percent you earn is usually taxable. If you apply the same tax rate, you will have an after-tax earnings rate of 5.36 percent (.67 times 8). The two sides offset one another.

4. *A mortgage is a debt.* Investors are also encouraged by some advisers to refinance their homes. The purpose is to free up "idle" equity and put it to work. Remember, there is no such thing as idle equity, as long as you do not borrow it. Do not forget that getting your equity through refinancing means going into debt, and accompanying this is interest expense. It simply may not fit your investment standards to go into debt in the first place, whatever the tax benefits and consequences of borrowing money secured by your home equity.

5. *In some cases, not borrowing is the wisest use of money.* Investors are under constant pressure to act at once and to make decisions.

ACTION CHECKLIST

Leverage

1. Never pay more in interest than you earn in profit.
2. Be aware, not only of the potential for gains from leverage, but also of the risks.
3. Evaluate total returns for leveraged and unleveraged strategies.
4. Keep your perspective when it comes to debt and investments. Be sure you know the risks before you take them.

There are many choices, many decisions to make, and everyone has a great idea. To take advantage and not miss the opportunity, you are told, you should borrow money. However large your list of choices might be, add one more choice to the list: *not* borrowing. That may be the wisest investment move you could make. It all depends on your standards and your goal. But if the risks of the investment are too high, going into debt will affect your cash flow and expose you to loss.

Avoiding the Tax Mistake

Make rules for yourself and follow them. Avoid the common investment errors by observing these guidelines:

1. *Plan year-round.* Recognize the importance of planning, not just at the end of the year, but as a year-round process. Employ planning as an investment strategy. Maintaining a portfolio is not limited to reviewing your holdings and buy or sell decisions; it also includes managing your tax status. That could mean reducing the tax burden or taking profits in a timely way and accepting the liability that results.

2. *Invest for profits, not taxes.* Seek profits and growth of capital rather than tax reduction or tax-free status. For example, if municipal bonds are not appropriate for your goals and investment standards, it is a mistake to purchase them just because they are exempt from tax. If you do not have passive gains, it is a mistake to invest in programs that will generate passive losses (because you will not be able to use them). And any buy or sell decision should be made first on the basis of investment timing, with taxes a secondary consideration.

3. *Be aware of the good and the bad side of deferral.* Deferral produces profits in a growing portfolio and is appropriate for many goals. However, when you cash in the investment, there *will* be a tax liability. In some cases, too, you will be penalized for withdrawing money before retirement. Be aware of how well deferral fits with the specific goals you set. Do not try to set up an emergency reserve fund, for example, in an account you cannot close out without penalty. Diversify not only between dissimilar products but also between liquid investment and deferred investments.

4. *Understand the tax implications of your investments.* Before investing money anywhere, be sure you understand how the rules work. Do not let yourself be distracted by low risk, high yield, or the

reputation of your plan's management. These are important tests, but you also need to know how the investment affects your income taxes.

5. *Seek professional help.* To ensure that you make the right decisions for yourself, you may need to consult with a tax accountant, attorney, or other specialist. Get your facts first. If a financial consultant offers tax advice, that might be appropriate, but only if he or she is qualified to explain the rules to you. If your adviser will earn a commission based on the investment decisions you make, be aware of the conflict. Use professional help aimed at providing you with advice in *your* best interests.

Records to Keep

Successful investors have a clear understanding and focus. They understand the risks of borrowing and of operating with a tax motive. They also know that in order to verify the transactions reported on their tax returns, they need to keep records.

The following are some guidelines for establishing your investment record-keeping system:

1. *Keep all the records in one place.* You may have all the records you need to verify what you claimed on your tax return, but if you are questioned, do you know how to lay your hands on what you will need? Keep an efficient, easily maintained system in one place. In that one location, set up a series of file folders containing *all* of your investment records: confirmations, brokerage statements, worksheets you develop on your own, annual statements from companies, contracts, research information—anything and everything related to your portfolio.

   Also record important information about your finances, especially if you are the only family member involved in managing your investments. Remember that, if you died suddenly, someone unfamiliar with your records would have a difficult time sorting out a haphazard system. List account numbers, holdings, bank account locations and numbers, and other information someone would need to figure out your portfolio.

2. *Summarize your profits and losses with a running record for the year.* Effective tax planning requires that you know how much profit or loss accumulates throughout the year. Record transactions from all of your investments as buy and sell orders are placed or as you receive confirmations and monthly statements. Keep track

of purchase date and amount, sale date and amount, and profit
or loss.

3. *Know how long you need to keep records.* Certain records have to be
   kept for a specified number of years. Be aware of how long you
   are expected to maintain records in your file. When deadlines
   have passed, destroy the older records to keep your system as
   lean as possible.

   Generally, you must keep tax verification records for three
   years from your filing deadline. For example, records for 1992
   should be kept until April 15, 1996, since the tax return's due date
   is April 15, 1993.

   If you request an extension for filing your tax return, the retention date is also extended. So if your filing deadline is pushed
   forward to August 15, you will need to retain your portfolio records for three years from that date.

   Some records will have to be kept much longer. These include
   contractual agreements for tax-deferred accounts, purchase dates
   for long-term investments, and records related to the purchase
   and sale of a residence.

4. *If you are not sure, do not throw it away.* It is better to keep more than
   you need than to throw out essential statements, reports, or confirmations. One investor, aware of the three-year retention rule,
   destroyed confirmations from her brokerage firm for stock purchases made. However, she did not sell the stock until later. In
   order to verify the net profit, she should have kept both the
   purchase and sales confirmation for three years after the sale
   date.

   Many records can be reproduced if destroyed by mistake. Your
   brokerage firm can supply copies of confirmations or monthly
   statements, and mutual fund companies can report transaction
   dates from the past. However, when you request copies, it will
   take time to receive them, and you might find you are missing
   essential records when you are up against a filing deadline.

Taxes are unavoidably connected to planning, goal setting, and the estab-
lishment of personal rules. You need to develop a comprehensive strategy for deferring taxes, earning a profit, and reaching your goals without
excessive risk. The next section offers guidelines on these topics.

SECTION SIX

Launching Your New Strategy

CHAPTER 16

Setting Your Immediate Goals

Successful people—investors as well as others—are goal-setters. They define and set specific goals for themselves, and they then take actions to meet them.

If this sounds like a simple idea, it really is. There is no great mystery involved in the process of thinking in terms of achievement. Once you have a goal or a series of goals and you know the direction you are going, you will have an easier time getting there. You will never reach every goal you set, but the ratio of successes to failures improves once you begin using this strategy.

This chapter discusses *short-term goals* (with deadlines of about a year), and the next chapter discusses those with longer periods in mind.

Goal-Setting Pitfalls

Once you begin setting goals and seeing the positive results from that process, you will realize that it is a sensible and obvious way to proceed. People who have experienced the satisfaction of being in control continue to set goals in every aspect of their life. It becomes a healthy habit and strategy.

Of course, there are pitfalls, and you should be aware of them before beginning to apply the goal-setting approach:

1. *Achieving the end result is not always as satisfying as the process of getting there*. People who actively practice goal-setting techniques soon discover that the satisfaction comes, not from reaching the goal, but from the process of setting and working toward it. As you get closer to actual completion and realization of the goal, there is a tendency to lose interest. For some, reaching the goal is actually a letdown.

   To solve this problem, plan future goals in advance. Once you see that the current goal will soon be reached, shift your emphasis to the new one.

   Example: Six months ago you set a goal to begin saving money to accumulate a fund equal to three months' salary. This is your emergency reserve fund. In reviewing your status this month, you see that this goal will be reached within a few weeks. It is time to set the next goal and move forward. The current goal will be completed, but you need to look ahead to the next step in your program.

2. *Goals will definitely change in the future.* It is rarely possible to set a short-term goal and do no further review work. Because it is short-term, you must expect the whole situation to change in the near future. Reaching the goal will require establishing a new one. However, even before the goal is reached, you may need to modify your strategies.

   Modification may occur for a number of reasons. Your economic situation might change suddenly. The loss of a job, a promotion, or an unexpected inheritance would be among the events demanding an immediate review and revision of short-term goals.

   The markets and market status may also force a change in goals. For example, a sudden change in a bull or bear market will probably change the investment strategies for stock market investors.

   Goals will also change because of changes in your own life. A marriage or divorce, the birth of a child, the purchase or sale of a home, or an unexpected death will bring about a need to reevaluate short-term goals.

   Finally, your maturity and investing experience will affect goals, perhaps even making past goals obsolete. The more you learn, the more skilled you become at setting goals. So a high-priority goal at age 25 might be replaced completely by the time you are 30 or older, or when the nature of your goals changes because of other economic factors.

3. *You need to review and change goals regularly.* Even when conditions in your life do not change, you still need to institute a program of

regular review, for two reasons. First, short-term goals will be achieved within a few months, so you need to replace them with updated, newer ones. Second, a goal under way now might need to be changed or abandoned in a very short time. You might want to abandon one direction for any number of reasons, such as the discovery of a new short-term priority.

4. *Failure to reach goals may discourage you from taking chances in the future.* Nothing is as encouraging as success. But by the same argument, nothing will be as discouraging as failure. If you begin your program of setting short-term goals and do not succeed at first, you might not be inclined to try again. However, remember that the goal itself is only a guideline. Achieving the goal is not the important point; the benefit lies in the process of working toward that goal.

No one will successfully reach every goal he or she sets. The value of clear, well-defined goals is in what you discover and achieve while moving toward them. You learn to set the best possible direction and move toward the goal, whether the end result comes about or not. In some cases, discovering an error and reversing course is more valuable than reaching the goal itself.

In some instances, the best short-term goal is to take no action in the immediate future. For example, if you have positioned yourself so that nothing should be done for at least the next three months, your goal might be to leave it alone. For some, this is the most difficult of all short-term goals. There is a tendency to want to be involved in making decisions, even when there is nothing to do for now.

The Power of Goals

You do not gain an advantage merely by identifying your short-term goals. The benefit of a goal orientation is the control it gives you. When you have a goal, you focus on the end result rather than simply react to the news and information of the moment. Then, when solicitations come your way, you evaluate them in terms of the goal and related investment standards—rather than being compelled to respond to something that you are told is "worthwhile" or that represents an "opportunity."

Can you control your future? Some investors, having subscribed to one system or another, are convinced that success is a matter of formula. Others believe that outcomes cannot be predicted and that the entire process is random. The debate applies to the stock market more than to other products or pools, but proponents of fundamental and technical systems believe firmly that their way works.

There is another method of thinking about the short-term future, one that demonstrates the degree of control you have. Consider the four events that can happen today that will affect a future outcome:

1. *Setting a goal.* Deciding to take control and following up by setting a goal puts the future into motion. Your action, response, and attitude will all be affected by the existence of the goal.

    Example: You set a goal last month to diversify your portfolio. For several years, you had intended to shift assets to diversify, but you had never gotten around to taking action. Then, as soon as you set the goal, the appropriate steps seemed to fall into place. Reaching the desired end result was much easier than you thought.

2. *Not setting a goal.* Your future is equally affected if you operate without a short-term goal. The lack of specific direction means that you have less self-guidance in responding to new information, selecting the right direction, and working toward a tangible result.

    Example: You have set standards for yourself, you have a good general idea of appropriate and acceptable risk levels, and you know what you want in the distant future. However, in response to telephone solicitations, advice from friends, or your stockbroker, you often make decisions that contradict your own policies. Your future is being affected because you do not have any specific short-term goals.

3. *Reaching a goal.* By reaching a plateau you planned and set into motion, you will have directly and decisively determined part of your future. You will not experience success with every goal; what matters is that you improve the ratio of success.

    Example: You have invested money many times in the past and have made decisions in a variety of ways. But now you have set a goal to run down a checklist of selection criteria before making any decisions. Now, when you are pressured to act quickly or "lose out on the opportunity," you refuse to respond. You want answers first, even if that means delaying your decision. You have reached the goal of using a methodical approach, and it leads to more success.

4. *Not reaching a goal.* Your future will also change when you do not reach a goal. A few minor failures should be accepted as part of an overall plan for greater success. For each failure, your future may change in one of two ways. First, you might abandon your approach. Second, you might learn from the experience of missing the goal, and then your future performance will improve. Both could occur at the same time, too.

> *Example:* You set a goal for yourself last year to invest $100 per month in a money market fund, with the idea of accumulating a liquid fund for short-term investments. However, the money has not been available lately, and the goal has gone dormant. In evaluating, you realize you do not have the capital to regularly invest this amount in addition to the other savings you are achieving. In response, you set a more realistic goal for yourself.

All of these possibilities and outcomes have one element in common: In each case, the action or lack of action demonstrates degrees of control. The more control you hold over today's events, the more control you have over your future.

Setting Investment Policies

A goal, by itself, does not lead to the success you want to achieve. You also need to establish a deadline and a set of policies that will help you meet your goal. These dictate a program you can follow and discipline you to take actions at the appropriate moment.

Your goals represent what you want, and they also reflect your perception of risk. But you must also apply investment standards to define risk, to select products, and to avoid mistakes. The methods you use in managing your portfolio demonstrate how well or how poorly you are able to control your own financial plan. Here are some illustrations of investment policies:

> *Example:* You have instructed the management of your mutual fund company to reinvest all income in additional shares.

> *Example:* You use a small portion of your total capital to speculate in the stock market. You always identify a price at which you will sell, either to take profits or to bail out of a losing situation.

Example: You receive a large number of telephone calls from commodities companies or stockbrokers. Each call offers big rewards. However, you are able to cut the calls short by explaining your policies: You never buy over the telephone, and you already have an adviser you use for all transactions.

All of these are policies. They limit or define your response and your action. Consider setting one absolute rule for yourself: Once you have decided on your own policies and once you are sure they work, you will not violate them. You may decline advice offered from others, for example, when it violates your rules to act. But the rules will also work only if you are able to follow them yourself. With a clear list of rules and policies, your decision-making process becomes very simple. You will reach more of your goals, and you will not be forced into making decisions on the moment: You will live by your own guidelines.

The process of setting goals while controlling your financial plan has several parts:

1. *Establish and define overall policies.* Always know where you are going. With goals in mind, you can tell which decisions of the moment will either fit or not fit your master plan. Just as corporate policies are necessary for order in a company, so personal investment policies are needed to truly manage your money. If you do not set policies, you can only react. You end up investing because someone brings an idea to you, which often means taking a direction contrary to the one you need.
2. *Set short-term goals and deadlines.* "Short-term" will mean a different time period for each person. It could be three months or an entire year. Regardless of how you define short-term, set goals and always assign a deadline to yourself. The combined goal and deadline disciplines you to structure and organize yourself.
3. *Seek suitable investments.* Once you have clear policies and goals in place, it is much easier to find the best investments for yourself. The vast majority of situations will probably be inappropriate for one narrowly defined goal. For example, if you are working on creating an emergency reserve fund, your investments should be highly liquid. So when a stranger telephones to tell you about an "exciting new limited partnership opportunity," you will know at once that it is not for you. The details of the program are of no interest. You know what you need, and the partnership just does not fit the program.
4. *Make valid comparisons.* When comparing two or more investments that seem to fit your short-term goal, be sure to make a valid

---
A C T I O N   C H E C K L I S T

Investment Policies

1. Establish investment policies and live by them.
2. Set goals and deadlines that conform to your policies.
3. Make sure all comparisons and evaluations are factual and valid.
4. Modify your goals constantly.

---

comparison. Do not concentrate just on yield. Be aware of the attributes of each choice, including risk level, liquidity, track record, and sensitivity to market changes. For example, suppose you are reviewing two bonds. One yields 11 percent, and the other yields only 7 percent. But the higher-yielding bond is also a greater risk. A comparison of yields alone is not valid.

5. *Review and modify.* Once you set a goal and a deadline, the very next step is to review both. As time passes, how is the goal working out? Are you moving toward completion? Is the goal still valid? What changes should be made? One of the most important steps in the process is to recognize when a goal should be abandoned or modified. Rarely can you set a short-term goal and then just leave it intact. You will always be in a process of review and change.

Defining What You Want

You may think of goal setting as a strategy or formula for consistently earning a profit. Although that is true, it is only part of the larger picture. Goals also force you to define carefully what you really want.

In some cases, setting a goal shows you that you have not yet defined what you need, that you have not yet taken this critical step. In trying to decide what your goal should be, you could find out that there is still more work to do beforehand.

This often happens when a husband and wife try to decide how and where to invest their money. In too many cases, the issues are not properly discussed before decisions are made; as a consequence, there is no agreement as to what the goal is. And sometimes the same words are used, but they mean two different things. Some financial planners working with couples use this technique: They ask each spouse to answer a few questions to define their goals. Then the answers are compared, and gaps in communication are identified. This makes it possible to clarify and to then move to the next step, finding suitable goals for both people. A test should include these questions:

1. How long is short-term?
2. How long is long-term?
3. What types of investors are we? Speculative, moderate, conservative?
4. How much monthly income will we need when we retire?
5. What is the most important feature that makes an investment safe?
6. Where should we be investing most of our money?
7. What is our most important short-term goal?
8. What is our most important long-term goal, and when will we achieve it?

Most couples who take this test discover at least one area of complete disagreement. That opens the door to discussion and agreement—or to acceptance of the fact that the two people have significantly different perceptions of how the process should work. For example, one spouse might say, "I never want to invest in bonds. They're too risky." The other might respond, "No, we should invest in *safe* bonds because there's very little risk."

Without clarification, one spouse or the other will end up making the decisions. The goals that spouse sets might be completely wrong for the other, or it will at least be perceived as wrong. But setting goals and then discussing them helps define what you want. It clarifies an unspoken disagreement and adds to your perception of the investment process.

Tax Deferral in Your Portfolio

The experience of setting goals and defining them as you proceed is a rewarding and comforting one. Your perspectives on investing change. No longer is it a mysterious or arbitrary environment in which luck is the key factor. No longer do you need to depend on the mystery of what someone else appears to know.

In developing your policies and instituting a procedure based on goals, you will need to consider profit potential, risk levels, diversification, liquidity, and financial restrictions. For the current year, you will also need to keep one eye on tax liabilities and include a periodic tax review. You might conclude that some of your capital should be invested in tax-deferred products or in a tax-deferred account.

To help define your goals, keep these questions in mind relating to tax deferral:

1. *Does tax deferral fit your goals?* It would be a mistake to position your entire portfolio in a tax-deferred environment only to delay tax liabilities. Your goals should dictate how much money should be invested in a deferred account, or even whether or not it is appropriate to do so.

2. *Do you have adequate liquidity?* By its nature, a tax-deferred investment in probably very illiquid. Withdrawing capital results in immediate taxation and, in many cases, a penalty as well. With this in mind, you should establish the liquidity you need before embarking on a tax-deferred program. An adequate amount is often represented by a number of months of take-home pay or a fixed amount that you can take to use for unexpected expenses. Set up your liquid fund before seeking tax-deferred investments.

3. *Do you need tax deferral?* You tax situation might not be so severe that you need to defer tax liabilities. If you are earning a relatively low income this year, you will pay taxes at a fairly low rate; in that case, do you need to tie up money in a tax-deferred account? It could make more sense to maximize return and flexibility now to build an equity base for the future. Then, when your overall income rises, you can change the goal and seek tax deferral. And remember, the taxes you defer today will eventually come due. If your tax bracket is going to be higher in the future, deferring liabilities today could result in more taxes later.

4. *How will changing goals affect the program?* When you begin a tax-deferral program today, it is based on the goals you establish now. But what will happen next year if your goals change? Will that make tax deferral a poor strategy? You cannot anticipate every possible change in future thinking, but you should be aware that deferral is a long-term strategy. Be aware that changing income, personal goals, and market conditions could change the attractiveness of tax deferral.

5. *How long a deferral period do you need?* The period of time you defer your tax liability will affect the goals you set. For example, you might have two separate goals: to save up money for a down-payment on a home within five years, and to begin putting money away for retirement in 35 years. Each of these goals demands a different deferral method.

The question of tax deferral forces you to think in terms of both short-term and long-term goals. The strategies you employ for long-term goals will be much different than those used to reach short-term goals. These strategies are explained in the next chapter.

CHAPTER 17

Working Toward Long-Term Goals

Some investors are never able to get beyond the problems of formulating short-term goals. They may be aware of the need for long-term planning, but they cannot get their program started. This problem occurs for a number of reasons. Most often investors are unable to get beyond short-term errors and never figure out how to build an essential base. Even when you are able to move from short-term to long-term goals, you need to apply a range of new and different strategies to keep your long-term goals on track.

Today's Actions and the Future

Before taking any action concerning a *long-term goal* (longer than a year), you need to first decide on the goal itself, the deadline, and how you can best achieve the desired result. This is a problem when two people are involved in the decision. For example, if two married people are in conflict on the essential questions of what they want to achieve, any action taken today will be inappropriate for one or for both.

Example: Two people are about to purchase their first home. In discussing financing terms and alternatives, the husband states that they need a 30-year loan and that they cannot afford a shorter repayment term. The wife insists they must finance the purchase

209

over 15 years because that is when they plan to retire; they want to repay their debt in full by that deadline.

In this example, a husband and wife have vastly different ideas about long-term goals. Both have valid points of view. But until their conflict is resolved, the proper way to achieve the goal cannot be resolved, since the actions they take today will affect their future. Will those actions create a cash problem? Will the decision prevent retirement by the target date? Is there a conflict between two future goals?

The couple in the example want to repay their mortgage loan in the future; they have also targeted a retirement date. It may be that both goals cannot be reached by the assigned deadlines. In this case, today's decisions have to be made with both goals in mind. Is there a compromise point? Is one goal a higher priority than the other? Should one or both long-term deadlines be changed?

Some long-term goals might seem realistic when first set and later prove to be less than feasible. In that case, the plan has to be modified. Either the month-to-month strategies must be changed or the goal has to be extended, abandoned, or changed.

> *Example:* A number of years ago, a family began putting money away for its child's college education. The child will graduate from high school this year and wants to attend a very expensive school in the fall. There is no scholarship money available, and the fund the family has been saving falls short of the four-year requirement by a large amount.

In this situation, some compromises are possible, but not all will be acceptable. The most drastic is to tell the child to find a different school. The least drastic is to expect the child to work part-time during the school year and full-time during the summer to help pay the bills. Many families refinance their homes or cash in other investments. In each situation, the amounts involved, the willingness of the child to participate in paying the bills, and the family's net worth will determine the most reasonable compromise or solution course.

The same problems may arise for any long-term goal. When the goal has been set many years in advance, its realization might require a last-minute adjustment for new realities.

> *Example:* More than a decade ago, you began saving money so you could start your own retail business and retire from your job. You based estimates on the cost of inventory, rent, and other

expenses at the time you began. Now, though, everything costs more and your investment capital is far from enough.

In this case, you have several alternatives: You could defer the goal to a later date, cash in some other investments, refinance your home, or apply for a business loan. The goal itself has not failed entirely; it just involved miscalculations. You need to modify it because the situation has changed.

Long-Term Tax Deferral

Tax deferral is often a practical strategy for long-term goals. Short-term ideas, in comparison, will probably change from one tax year to the next, so that any significant deferral will not produce benefits making it worthwhile in the short term.

As this book has shown, some investments come with built-in deferral features. For example, if you invest in capital assets, you control the timing of the sale and, as a result, the year that taxes become due.

> *Example:* Among your investments are shares of stock in a number of companies, which have increased in value during the past year. You also own your own home, and its market value has increased because of rising prices in your area.

In cases of capital asset investment, the growth that has been realized is not taxed until the asset is sold. So stock, real estate, and any other asset falling into this category are within your control to time and plan. Deferral is a controllable and basic feature.

Each investment and its underlying value should be matched to the applicable long-term goal. This is the point that is so often missed. For example, you might find yourself considering putting your home on the market only because it has increased in value and can be sold for a substantial profit. But why sell now? Do you want to move? Do you need a bigger or a smaller house? Or are you merely reacting to the idea of taking profits while you can?

Unless you are motivated by the realization of a specific goal, the decision will not make sense. A long-term investor should not react to the immediate temptation to sell a home or shares of stock held for the long term. And yet that sort of action is taken frequently.

When you match the investment to the goal, tax deferral and its advantages become readily apparent. For example, if you are saving for a child's education in 15 years, it will make more sense to accumulate funds through a tax-deferred annuity, savings bonds, or an IRA than it would to save in a taxable account. The overall compound return will be much greater when the tax liability is deferred.

You may also be aware that a number of different goals within your portfolio are in conflict with one another. So how do you coordinate dissimilar long-term goals, especially when some are tax-deferred and others are not? The answer is to divide the portfolio, either allotting specific dollar amounts to each investment, or setting aside portions for each long-term goal. It is probably more likely that each long-term goal you set will require accumulation of a specific amount on a regular basis.

> *Example:* You have a number of long-term goals. You have tar-geted a retirement date in 35 years, and you plan to repay your mortgage debt within 27 years. You also have two children, and you are saving for their college education in 14 and 11 years.

Each of these goals may be met by contributing a fixed amount per month in a specific manner. Your retirement funds could be invested in long-term, deferred accounts; the mortgage debt is being repaid with nondeferred money (but home equity is accumulating and will not be taxed until the house is sold); and a college fund can be set up in a deferred account, with target dates in mind.

All of the goals in the example can benefit from tax deferral. Deferral works for most long-term goals; it probably fails to work only when you are not sure whether the goal will change in the immediate future. In other words, deferral may be a questionable strategy until the goal is firmed up.

Diversifying for the Long Term

Most investors understand the basic principle of diversification: Assets are spread around among enough different accounts or types of invest-ments that a shift in the various markets will not adversely affect the whole picture. However, this principle may take on a different character when your portfolio includes both short-term and long-term invest-ments and when you have a number of different goals in mind.

By their nature, short-term investments do not contain many of the important attributes of longer-term ones. Tax deferral is the most obvious of these attributes. The balance of a portfolio between short- and long-term will vary, depending on the amount of money involved, the period you have been managing the account, and the nature of all of your goals.

The short-term side of your portfolio may take up most or all of your portfolio until you have built up enough capital to add in the longer-term element. In this situation, you can still achieve diversification with long-term planning in mind. Some suggestions are as follows:

1. *Begin with mutual fund accounts.* The easiest way to diversify with a limited amount of capital is through a mutual fund, which is diversified by nature. However, each fund has its own investment policy or objective. If you are seeking safety and moderate risk, be sure you do not place your capital in a high-risk, high-yield fund.

   Also consider a money market mutual fund for current income with diversification. Whether you are building toward the development of longer-term goals or just looking for an account in which to temporarily leave funds, you can use the money market account as a convenience in your portfolio.

2. *Budget long-term investments.* Even if you are not yet ready to embark on a full-scale financial plan, you can begin to deposit some money into a long-term account. For example, you might not be ready to put a large amount down on a real estate investment, but you may be able to start depositing $50 per month in a tax-deferred IRA account.

   When you budget long-term investment funds, you build a portfolio base for the future. You may not have a permanent long-term goal in mind yet. But when you do come up with one, you will have a head start if you have been budgeting each year.

3. *Diversify, not just by investment type, but also by yield.* Do not make the mistake of thinking about diversification only as it applies to products. Another form of diversification is achieved when you vary your portfolio yield.

   Example: You have a sum of money in a passbook savings account. You want and need liquidity, but you have more than you need. Half of that 6 percent money could be moved to an 8 percent certificate and tied up for six months. That gives you a yield diversification. You have the liquidity you need, and you are earning an average of 7 percent on the entire amount.

A Goals Checklist

In order to pick long-term investments appropriate for your own goals, remember these guidelines:

1. *Invest specifically for each long-term goal.* Once you have properly and completely defined a long-term goal, you will know when

you need to accumulate funds, as well as how much. For example, a child's college education is a future event with a deadline and an amount (based on today's prices and assumptions about future changes).

You should match your investments to each long-term goal, recognizing that not all are the same. For example, you may put *all* your investment capital in a growth mutual fund, assuming that it will be adequate for a list of future goals. However, you might be able to defer or even avoid taxes on a portion of this capital by coordinating the investment with long-term goals and by finding other places to invest.

2. *Calculate tax and inflation factors.* One problem with setting long-term goals is that you cannot know the future. Your assumptions must be based on what you know today about tax rates, deferral rules, interest rates, and costs. If a child's college education in 15 years is much more expensive than you calculated, you will have a financial problem in the future. And if the rate of increase in housing prices is greater than the compound savings rate on your investments, you will never have enough for a down-payment.

In comparing taxable and tax-deferred investments, include a tax comparison in the exercise. Make certain you are comparing the after-tax yield for investments with similar safety features. Also remember to add in an inflation factor. Just as the yield you earn may be compounded every year, so inflation should be figured for its compound effect.

3. *Aim for long-term deadlines.* You really do not have a long-term goal until you also have a deadline. Saying you would like to start your own business, buy a home, or retire "one day" does not point the way toward achieving the goal. You need to impose a deadline on yourself.

Most long-term goals are extremely specific. You know when you want to retire or pay off your home. You know when your children will reach college age. And you probably know when you could have the investment funds available to execute those goals.

4. *Use long-term selection strategies.* Avoid buying and selling investments like a speculator when you need to think far ahead. This is a problem for anyone who has become accustomed to thinking only like a short-term strategist.

For example, you may receive a telephone call from a stockbroker, who recommends a "hot" stock, or a stock that will rise in the near future. You therefore buy 200 shares. If that stock does rise in value, you will be able to sell and make a profit. But if you use long-term funds to do this, what have you done?

First, you have used long-term capital to speculate. What if the stock falls in value? Can you afford the risk? Second, the decision was not appropriate because the money was marked as long-term. You might want to invest in the stock market, but it is better, with long-term money, to pick companies with the best future growth potential, not just the possibility of higher market value in the next six months.

5. *Review the long-term portfolio from a long-term point of view.* Reacting and responding in a short-term manner is one common mistake. Another is forgetting to review the portfolio with a long-term point of view.

   This is an easy trap to fall into, because we are told time and again to take profits when they are earned. So you may have a portfolio of stocks or mutual fund shares that have increased in value over the past five years. You are tempted to sell now and take your profits, before the trend is reversed. However, the long-term approach requires a different question: Are these investments still appropriate for the long-term goal? If they are, then they should not be cashed in.

6. *Time liquidity to match the goal deadline.* Liquidity—the availability of your capital when you need it—is generally associated with short-term investments. Yes, you want to be able to get your hands on an emergency reserve fund with as little delay as possible. For longer-term investments, the question of liquidity is too distant to be of immediate concern, but it *is* of long-term concern. In planning your long-term portfolio, you should be aware of liquidity and your deadline.

   Example: You know you will need that college fund money in 16 years, and you are thinking of investing in bonds. Why even consider bonds that will mature beyond 16 years? By doing so, you risk losing part of your capital. If, at the end of 16 years, your bonds are deeply discounted, you will be forced to take a loss to get your money back.

7. *Seek professional help when needed.* Putting together a comprehensive portfolio, including short-term and long-term elements, and achieving the diversification and liquidity you know you need might be overwhelming and confusing. In that case, seek professional help. Locate a financial planner or adviser who will work with you and who will respect the goals and risk standards you explain.

   Professionals are aware of a wide range of products and the attributes of each. By using the services of a qualified planner or adviser, you will make your task much easier. But remember: Ultimately, you will have to make your own decisions, and you cannot expect someone else to tell you what is best.

The next chapter offers specific ideas for putting your strategy into action, including ways to locate and use information sources.

CHAPTER 18

How to Get Started

This book has examined a number of products and investment strategies, the question of risk, methods of making valid comparisons, and the all-important question of the tax consequences involved with every decision. While discussing all of these points, it has emphasized one underlying idea: Even though tax deferral makes sense in many cases, that should not be the motive for your decisions. Deferral is not a goal, but a benefit of proper planning and positioning.

All of the topics discussed so far should help you to define your priorities and control tax liabilities. However, the entire discussion is of little value unless you know where to find and compare tax-deferred investments. The truth is, tax deferral is occurring all around you. If you own any capital assets—a home, common stock, rare coins—any growth in value is tax-deferred until that asset is sold. If you have any money in an IRA, a Keogh account, or your employer's pension or profit-sharing plan, the earnings and, in many instances, the money contributed to the account are free of current taxes.

The problem is not finding deferred investments; it is deciding which ones to include in your portfolio. Beyond those investments with built-in deferral features, such as annuities or Series EE bonds, virtually any investment can be purchased in such a way that income is deferred.

Examples: You have a large sum of money invested in a taxable money market fund. Interest income of several thousands of dollars per year is earned. If that account is held as part of an IRA or other qualified retirement plan, you will not be taxed on interest until funds are withdrawn.

Using Brokers and Financial Advisers

You can seek information about products through a number of sources. One readily available source is your own broker. If you invest in the stock market, your broker might be the most obvious source. After all, he or she handles transactions in stocks, mutual funds, and bonds, and may even be able to establish an IRA.

Generally, however, a broker might not be the person to consult for every type of tax-deferred investment, for the simple reason that you can get many of the safest and simplest tax-deferred products without paying a sales commission. Unfortunately, your broker earns a living from selling on commission, so he or she will not always propose products like Series EE bonds and tax-free money market accounts. Still, your broker might be able to offer alternatives for diversifying your portfolio, for finding the most practical form of IRA or Keogh account, or getting other information on tax deferral.

Financial planners or advisers may be helpful sources as well. A word of caution, however: The planning industry is not regulated. Virtually anyone may use a title implying expertise in the financial services. There are a few methods you can use to distinguish the opportunists from the professionals:

1. *Designations.* Does the individual hold any professional licenses, such as CFP (certified financial planner) or ChFC (chartered financial consultant)? Having these letters behind a name does not guarantee or prove that these individuals are capable, but it does show that they have gone through a course of study, taken a test, and passed. Designations do not create professionals; however, professionals are more likely to have designations.
2. *Experience.* Always ask how many years a person has been in the business. Competent independent planners or advisers should have several years of experience, either in an apprenticeship with someone else or in their own on a related industry, such as brokerage or insurance.
3. *Range of product knowledge.* Some people use terms like *adviser* or *planner* in their title but in reality only sell one type of product. If your planner offers only life insurance or only mutual funds as

solutions to your personal planning needs, he or she is not in planning. Seek a professional who offers the widest possible range of investment and insurance products, either directly or through affiliated professionals.

4. *Approach.* Does your planner offer you a solution before you explain the problem? The sale should be the last step, coming only after a complete exploration of what you are trying to achieve. If someone recommends action without first exploring risk tolerance, your tax status and the possible need for deferral, and a definition of your personal goals, look elsewhere for help.

5. *Client list.* Who are the professional's other clients? Your adviser should be willing to provide you with the names, addresses, and telephone numbers of his or her other clients without any hesitation. Does your current status seem to match the list? In other words, are ages, income ranges, location, and other factors similar? You may want to work with a professional most familiar with your lifestyle and economic status.

   Also ask these questions:

   "How would your recommendation be different for someone earning twice as much income per year?"

   The adviser should be able to distinguish clearly between different recommendations, and his or her answer should be based on the attributes of a particular client.

   "What types of investors do *not* need to defer income taxes?"

   The answer should show the adviser's knowledge of the impact of taxation on total return and on net worth.

6. *Fee policies.* Some financial professionals earn both commissions and fees. A fee-based adviser is required to disclose to you exactly how the fee is computed; if offering consultation services for a fee, the person should also be affiliated with a registered investment adviser and should comply with the (SEC) regulations for charging fees.

Other Information Sources

You do not need to depend entirely on brokers and financial planners to gain information about tax-deferred investing. Remember, a large number of the best tax-deferred investments are available without any sales charges. Some other information sources you may want to use are the following:

Automated Networks and Data Bases

Many companies now offer automated online data bases, notably for stock market quotations. Charles Schwab and Company and Dow Jones both offer stock market programs designed for this purpose.

Detailed information beyond quotations and stock market news is available on a subscription basis through one of the several online services. Two of the largest specializing in investment information are Dow Jones News/Retrieval (P.O. Box 300, Princeton, NJ 08540) and Compu-Serve Information Services (500 Arlington Centre Boulevard, Columbus, OH 43220).

Research Services

Several companies provide market research, often in very narrowly focused industries, product types, or even regions. These services are available by subscription. Two services oriented to the stock market include The Outlook, published by Standard & Poor's Corporation (25 Broadway, New York, NY 10004), and The Value Line Investment Survey (711 Third Avenue, New York, NY 10017).

Other specialized research is best located by studying publications devoted to the specific industry. For example, in the mutual fund industry, a large number of newsletters and research services may help. An industry membership organization, the Investment Company Institute (1775 K Street NW, Washington, DC 20006) publishes a listing of its membership and informational brochures.

You may also write to the Consumer Information Center (P.O. Box 100, Pueblo, CO 81002) and ask for a free copy of the *Consumer Information Catalog*. This lists many free and low-cost books, booklets, and brochures for investors.

Industry Newsletters

If you plan to conduct research through newsletters, you face a big problem. How do you know which of the hundreds of investment newsletters will give you the information you need? One solution is to take a trial subscription to a number of newsletters. Select Information Exchange (SIE) is a company that offers packages of trial subscriptions to a number of different publications. Generally, the trial period runs about six weeks, long enough to see whether the newsletter is right for you.

The benefit of trial subscriptions is exposure to a wide range of information. The big disadvantage is that your name and address end up on a number of other lists. You will receive information you did not ask for, and it will take a while for your name to disappear from the secondary lists. Contact SIE for a free catalog describing trial subscriptions currently available (2095 Broadway, New York, NY 10023).

Financial Newspapers and Magazines

The most widely read financial newspapers are *The Wall Street Journal* and *Barron's*. Both are published by Dow Jones (200 Burnett Road, Chicopee, MA 01021). Another widely read financial paper is *Investor's Daily*, which provides detailed stock market ratings and comparisons (P.O. Box 25970, Los Angeles, CA 90025).

A number of specialized business and investment magazines may be useful as well, not so much for updating current information as for background. Magazines published weekly may prove the most valuable. Remember that the articles in monthly or quarterly magazines were probably prepared 30 to 180 days before they appeared.

Magazines include *Fortune, Forbes, Inc., Business Week,* and *Financial World.* For less orientation on business and more on individual investing, also consider *Changing Times* and *Money.*

Investor Associations

Another information source especially valuable for new investors is the association. A regional or national organization may be able to offer literature or access to other investors, seminars and classes, or discounts on services.

Two national organizations worth investigating are the American Association of Individual Investors, or AAII (625 North Michigan Avenue, Chicago, IL 60611) and the National Association of Investors Corporation, or NAIC (1515 Eleven Mile Road, Royal Oak, MI 48067). The AAII is a nonprofit organization with 100,000 members and chapters in 43 cities. It publishes a journal and offers discounts on other publications. The NAIC has approximately 125,000 members and specializes in helping individuals form and operate investment clubs. The organization supplies literature and publications as well as its own magazine.

Identifying the Real Risks

This book has mentioned and examined the idea of risk in many variations. However, one risk you constantly face while trying to set goals, stay on course, and control your financial future is knowledge risk. You need to update your knowledge continuously to seek new information and rules about investment products, the economy, and the tax law. You will probably need help from an investment expert as well as an accountant or other tax preparer.

The more knowledge you acquire and the more faithfully you keep it up to date, the better you will be able to control your own investments and to reach the goals you have set. Any investor who makes a series of assumptions and then fails to review them within a year is bound to make mistakes. A new job, a change in family size or status, a raise, a new tax law, market condition, or regulatory change—all these demand a review of everything.

When you have gathered information and identified the sources best suited for your portfolio, you have reached the plateau necessary to put your goals into action. You will have a clear course and know exactly how to begin. If the economy or the markets change, you can then react with a focused, methodical approach, and never on impulse or without a full understanding of the risks you face.

You also know whether or not tax deferral is an essential strategy today or just a good idea to be used in the future. You have gotten away from the pitfall of making investment decisions for tax reasons. You know how to plan for tax liabilities and how to time and position your accounts to work within the law and avoid surprises.

Change is inevitable. The difference, you discover, is that by staying in touch and diligently keeping track, you are able to adjust to change as it occurs instead of just reacting to it afterwards. Now you are directing your portfolio and not being led by circumstances. That gives you the power to realize your goals, and that is the financial power we all want and deserve.

Glossary

abusive tax shelter A program designed to reduce or eliminate tax liabilities rather than to provide the investor with economic value.

accelerated cost recovery system (ACRS) The method of depreciation introduced in the 1980s, in which a finite number of recovery periods and asset classifications were introduced.

accelerated depreciation Depreciation that is greater than straight-line during the earlier years and lower in future years.

active investor An investor meeting the qualifications under tax law to write off current-year losses without the restrictions of passive losses. The individual must own no less than 10 percent of a property or program and must have the power to make decisions regarding tenants, leases, rents, and management.

adjusted basis The basis in property consisting of purchase price, costs of purchase, plus any capital improvements and less allowable depreciation.

after-tax profit The true net profit earned from investing, derived by deducting that portion of the profit that must be paid in current federal, state, and local income taxes from the gross profit.

alternative minimum tax (AMT) An additional tax imposed on individuals reporting preference items or claiming deductions of certain types. The purpose of the AMT is to ensure that all taxpayers will incur a liability for some level of tax and that seeking preference items will not completely eliminate a liability.

amortization schedule   The schedule showing the time and payment amounts required to retire a loan by the agreed-upon year; this schedule is based on the amount borrowed, the interest rate in effect, and the compounding method used.

annual compounding   A method of computing compound interest in which interest is figured once per year and added to a previous balance in an account.

annuity   A contract between an insurance company and an individual owner. In exchange for payments given in a lump sum or a series, the insurer promises to make monthly payments once the owner reaches a specified age. The payments will continue for a specified number of years, until a specified amount has been paid out, or for life.

assumed inflation rate   The rate of inflation you believe will be in effect in the future, used to develop financial models and plans.

attribute   A feature of an investment which defines one or more forms of risk. An attribute, also referred to as a profile of an investment product, should not be confused with a goal.

blind pool program   A form of limited partnership in which specific properties are not identified at the time investment capital is raised. The organizers of the program outline an investment policy and describe the types of properties they will purchase. In comparison, a specified program is organized to purchase and manage one or more properties already identified.

breakeven interest rate   The rate of interest required to maintain the value of one's capital after deducting the consequences of taxes and inflation.

call   An option to buy 100 shares of stock at a fixed price and for a limited time. A covered call is one for which the seller also owns 100 shares of the stock.

capital asset   A long-term asset that can be depreciated, such as real estate or equipment held in business or an investment subject to capital gains or losses.

capital gain distributions   Payments made to shareholders of mutual fund accounts; these payments represent a capital gain realized from investment activity.

capital gain or loss   The gain or loss realized upon sale of a capital asset, distinguished from other gains or losses by annual loss limitations and, before the Tax Reform Act of 1986, by a different taxing rate.

compound interest   Interest earned when previously earned interest is added to the basis over more than one period.

decreasing term insurance   A form of term life insurance in which the annual premium remains the same for the entire coverage term but the amount of insurance in force declines over the period, reflecting changing levels of coverage based on the age of the insured person.

deferred annuity   An annuity contract in which a single deposit or a series of deposits are made over time and payments from the company to the individual are scheduled to begin in the future.

depreciation   The gradual writing off of business or investment capital assets over a period of time (called the recovery period). Depreciation uses the cost recovery system mandated under the law and is based on the year the asset was placed in service.

dividend   Payments to stockholders of part of the year's corporate profits. In a mutual fund account, a dividend may include both stock dividends and interest earned on debt securities in the portfolio.

EE bond   A series bond issued by the U.S. Treasury. The bond is purchased at one-half face value, and interest is credited twice per year. Income is not taxed annually but is deferred until the bond is cashed.

effective tax rate   The percentage of tax that is applied to any income earned above a plateau of taxable income at the top of each bracket for the current year.

equity REIT   A real estate investment trust formed to buy real estate.

equivalent yield   The taxable yield a bond investor needs to match the tax-exempt interest available from a municipal bond. To compute, divide the tax-exempt yield by the percentage remaining after deducting the tax rate from 100.

exclusion ratio   A calculation used to determine the portion of annuity benefits representing return of capital, which is free from tax, and the portion representing deferred income, which is taxable.

face amount   The amount of protection promised upon maturity.

finite-life REIT   A real estate investment trust formed with the intention to self-liquidate at a specified future date. Finite-life REITs are often formed for ten years.

fixed annuity   An annuity contract in which terms are fixed. In a fixed amount contract, the monthly payout is fixed, but the period will vary with the amount invested, the owner's age, and the insurance company's investment experience. In a fixed period contract, the duration of payouts is fixed, but the monthly payout varies.

401K plan   An employee profit-sharing plan with a salary reduction feature. Tax-deductible contributions are adjusted each year according to the cost of living index.

403B plan   A retirement account available to employees in education and not-for-profit companies. Proceeds contributed by employees (and often added to contributions made by the employer) are used to buy tax-deferred annuities. Annual maximum contribution levels are adjusted for cost-of-living increases.

future value of 1   The calculated value of a single deposit of money that is allowed to grow at an assumed rate of interest compounded in a specific manner.

future value of 1 per period   The calculated value of a series of deposits that are allowed to grow at an assumed rate of interest compounded in a specific manner.

goal   The desired end result of investing, or the purpose for which funds are being accumulated by a specific deadline.

HH bond   A series bond issued by the U.S. Treasury. The HH bond can be purchased only by transferring the value accumulated in a Series EE bond.

hybrid REIT   A real estate investment trust that may assume combinations of equity and debt investments in real estate.

immediate annuity   An annuity contract in which the owner gives the insurance company a single lump-sum payment. The contractual payouts normally begin immediately or within one year.

individual retirement account (IRA)   An account in which investment earnings are not taxed until funds are withdrawn. Some individuals are allowed to deduct IRA contributions of up to $2,000 per year; others may not claim the deduction but are allowed to defer profits on investments within the IRA.

inflation risk   The risk that the net value of a portfolio will decline in terms of real spending power because of inflation.

interest calculation   The multiplication of three factors: the principal amount, the interest rate, and time. The result of this calculation is the amount of interest.

Keogh plan   A qualified plan for self-employed individuals. A portion of annual net profits from self-exployment may be contributed to a

Keogh account, and the contributions may be deducted from reportable gross income. All investment earnings in the account are deferred until funds are withdrawn.

level term insurance   A form of term life insurance in which the face amount (insurance protection) remains the same throughout the contract term; however, annual premiums are raised periodically on the basis of the insured person's age.

life annuity   An annuity that guarantees payments for the rest of the annuitant's life.

limited partnership   An investment program in which the capital of many investors is pooled and placed under the management of general partners. The limited partners are not entitled to a voice in management decisions; however, their liability is limited to their at-risk investment position. In comparison, the general partners are exposed to unrestricted liability.

liquidity risk   The risk that one cannot get any cash from one's investments without accepting a loss in capital value.

long-term goal   An investing or personal goal whose deadline is planned for the distant future, generally beyond the coming 12 months.

market risk   The risk that the current market value of an investment will fall below the basis.

master limited partnership (MLP)   A real estate investment company that manages funds and properties for investors in real estate. Shares are traded publicly. However, unlike with stock mutual funds, the share value varies with current yield rather than with asset value.

modified accelerated cost recovery system (MACRS)   A system based on the accelerated cost recovery system, with updated rules concerning asset classifications and recovery periods for business and investment assets.

monthly compounding   A method of calculating compound interest. The nominal, or annual, rate is divided by 12. The fractional answer is applied as the monthly interest rate for each of 12 months during the year.

mortgage acceleration   The reduction of overall interest costs on a home mortgage, achieved by paying more than required toward the principal. The result is a reduction of the loan balance ahead of the amortization schedule, meaning significantly lower interest expense and more rapid payoff of the loan.

mortgage-backed security   An investment program organized into pools; a form of mortgage debt mutual fund. Such programs are offered by the Government National Mortgage Association ("Ginnie Mae") and the Federal National Mortgage Association ("Fannie Mae").

mortgage REIT   A real estate investment trust that invests capital in mortgages rather than in equity. The REIT program may specialize in secured first mortgages on existing properties, on construction financing, or on combinations of both.

municipal bond   A debt security issued by a state or local government or an agency of the government.

mutual fund   A managed pool in which the funds belonging to many investors are professionally used to achieve a specified objective (such as income or growth).

nominal interest rate   The stated rate of interest without regard for the compounding method. For example, a bond yields 8 percent per year, which is the nominal rate. However, because one-half of that rate is paid every six months, the annual yield is greater than the nominal interest rate.

nongovernmental purpose bond   A bond issued to finance activities not directly related to a public purpose of the municipality. Each issuer is limited in the amount of such bonds it may issue tax-free. Above that level, interest on the nongovernmental purpose bond is taxable at the federal level.

option   An intangible investment giving the right to buy or to sell stock for a fixed, specified price, and for a limited time.

over-55 exclusion   A provision in tax law allowing individuals over age 55 to exclude from taxes up to $125,000 in profits from the sale of a home. This provision is allowed only once for each person.

passive investment   Any investment in which the investor does not materially and directly participate. In such investments, any losses are deductible only to the extent that they offset passive activity gains reported in the same year.

period certain   The number of years over which payments will continue in an annuity contract when the contract specifies payments for a number of years rather than for life.

preference item   A form of income or loss that gives the taxpayer a deduction, deferral, faster write-off, or stepped-up basis in property beneficial to the tax situation. Many preference items are disallowed under the alternative minimum tax computation.

present value of 1   The single sum required to be placed on deposit today to reach a target amount in the future, assuming that interest will be accumulated at a specified rate and compounded in a specified manner.

present value of 1 per period   The amount required in a series of payments beginning today to fund a series of payments beginning in the future, assuming that interest will be accumulated at a specified rate and compounded in a specified manner.

pre-tax profit   The profit from an investment; the amount existing before the income taxes resulting from that profit are deducted.

pre-tax yield   The yield, or rate of return, of a taxable investment that is required to match the yield of a tax-deferred investment. To compute, subtract the effective tax rate from 100 to determine the after-tax rate. Next, divide the tax-deferred yield by the after-tax rate. The result is the required pre-tax yield in a taxable investment.

private activity bond   A bond issued by a municipality for nonessential activities. Such a bond is subject to federal income taxes.

public purpose bond   A municipal bond on which all income is exempt from federal income tax. A public purpose bond is issued to fund essential services of the municipality.

put   An option to sell 100 shares of stock at a fixed price and for a limited time.

qualified annuity   An annuity in which deposits are tax-dererred and all proceeds are taxed upon withdrawal.

quarterly compounding   A method of compounding interest. The annual rate is divided by 4. Interest is then calculated on the fractional rate and applied to the principal for each of four quarters during the year.

real estate investment trust (REIT)   A trust organized to invest in real estate programs. The REIT does not pay taxes, since no less than 95 percent of annual profits are passed through to investors and taxed at that level. Shares of beneficial interest in the REIT are traded publicly, like stock in a corporation.

recovery period   The number of years required to completely depreciate a business or investment asset. Recovery periods and depreciation methods are prescribed by tax regulations.

REIT in perpetuity   A real estate investment trust formed without a specific future date for liquidation. Such a program may exist indefinitely or may decide to liquidate in the future.

return of capital distribution   A payment, made by a mutual fund to shareholders, that represents a partial return of invested capital rather than a taxable payment of income or capital gains.

risk profile   The beliefs, limitations, and standards an individual investor develops to help locate and define appropriate investment products.

semiannual compounding   A method of compounding interest. The annual rate is divided by 2, and interest is paid or charged twice per year at the half-year rate.

shares of beneficial interest   The shares held by investors in real estate investment trusts. Such shares are similar to shares of stock in corporations. Each investor owns a beneficial interest in the total assets of the trust.

short-term goal   A personal investment or other personal goal set with a deadline in the immediate future, generally one year or less.

simple interest   The calculation of interest based solely on the principal amount and without any compounding over time.

simplified employee pension (SEP)   A retirement account for self-employed people or corporate employees. A specified percentage of income, up to an annual limit, is contributed each year in a tax-deferred account.

sinking fund payments   The amounts required to be deposited in a series of payments to reach a target amount in the future, assuming that interest will be accumulated at a specified rate and compounded in a specified manner.

specified program   A limited partnership formed to raise capital and to purchase one or more specific properties. In comparison, a blind pool program outlines an investment policy but does not identify the properties it will purchase.

straight-line depreciation   A form of depreciation in which the same amount is claimed each year over the recovery period.

tax deferral   The delay of a tax liability to a future year. Taxes can be deferred in three ways: by timing a sale, by placing investments in a qualified deferral vehicle, or by selecting investments which are not currently taxed.

tax-exempt investment   An investment whose income is exempt from taxation. In comparison, a tax-deferred investment's income is taxed at a later date.

Tax Reform Act of 1986   Major tax legislation that replaced the previous bracketing system with three tax brackets; revised depreciation methods, investment interest deductions, and passive loss limitations; and removed or restricted many itemized deductions.

tax shelter   In general, any investment that gives the investor favorable benefits through tax reduction. Specifically, a program designed and structured for tax benefits rather than for economic or investment value.

term life insurance   Life insurance which protexts the insured person for a specified term of years only and which includes no savings element. The amount of coverage may be level or decreasing. Under terms of a level term life insurance policy, premiums are raised on the basis of the insured person's age. Under terms of a decreasing term policy, the premium remains the same but coverage declines each year.

underlying stock   The stock on which a call or put option is held.

undistributed capital gain   A capital gain that is earned in a mutual fund account but that is not paid out or credited to shareholders' accounts. Instead, the value of the capital gain is used to increase each investor's basis in shares.

universal life insurance   An insurance company product that combines features of insurance and investment. A current investment rate is guaranteed each year. Part of a total premium is assigned to insurance protection, and the balance is invested. Within limitations, owners are allowed to increase the amount of insurance in force from one year to the next.

universal variable life insurance   An insurance company product combining certain features of universal life and variable life. Insured people have the right to alter the amount of insurance in force within specified annual limits. They also have control over their investment portfolios.

variable life insurance   An insurance company product combining features of whole life insurance and investment value. Variable life contracts are considered as securities and must by registered with the Securities and Exchange Commission (SEC). A minimum death benefit is guaranteed by contract, and the insured person directs investments in the account with excess funds.

wash sale rule   A tax rule stating that a 30-day waiting period must be applied before sold securities may be repurchased. If the securities are repurchased within 30 days, a loss will not be allowed on the sale.

whole life insurance   A form of life insurance in which two elements are combined: insurance and savings (cash value). The face value of the policy is predominantly insurance during the early years; as the maturity date approaches, the savings element grows and insurance coverage declines. By the time the policy matures, no insurance remains; the entire face amount is savings.

zero coupon bond   A bond purchased at a discount from face value. Investors do not receive interest payments based on nominal rates twice per year; instead, their basis in zero coupon bond issues rises during the holding period. At maturity, the face value of the bond is payable.

INDEX